MOBILE LEARNING MINDSET

THE COACH'S GUIDE TO IMPLEMENTATION

CARL HOOKER

International Society for Technology in Education
PORTLAND, OREGON • ARLINGTON, VIRGINIA

Mobile Learning Mindset
The Coach's Guide to Implementation
Carl Hooker

Editor: *Emily Reed*
Production Manager: *Christine Longmuir*
Copy Editor: *Kristin Landon*
Cover Design: *Brianne Beigh*
Book Design and Production: *Kim McGovern*

Library of Congress Cataloging-in-Publication Data available

First Edition
ISBN: 978-1-56484-375-3
Ebook version available

Printed in the United States of America

About ISTE

The International Society for Technology in Education (ISTE) is the premier nonprofit organization serving educators and education leaders committed to empowering connected learners in a connected world. ISTE serves more than 100,000 education stakeholders throughout the world.

ISTE's innovative offerings include the ISTE Conference & Expo, one of the biggest, most comprehensive ed tech events in the world—as well as the widely adopted ISTE Standards for learning, teaching and leading in the digital age and a robust suite of professional learning resources, including webinars, online courses, consulting services for schools and districts, books, and peer-reviewed journals and publications. Visit iste.org to learn more.

About the Author

Carl Hooker has been involved in education since graduating from the University of Texas in 1998. He has been in a variety of positions in both Austin Independent School District (ISD) and Eanes ISD, from first grade teacher to virtualization coordinator.

Hooker is now director of innovation and digital learning at Eanes ISD. He is also the founder of the learning festival iPadpalooza (http://ipadpalooza.com). As director, he uses his background in both education and technology to bring a unique vision to the district and its programs. During his tenure, Eanes has jumped into social media, adopted the Google Apps for Education, and started to build a paperless environment with Google Docs. Hooker helped spearhead the Learning and Engaging through Access and Personalization (LEAP) program, which put 1:1 iPads into the hands of all K–12 students at Eanes.

Hooker has been a part of a strong educational shift with technology integration. From his start as a teacher to his current district technology leadership role, he has always held one common belief: Kids need to drive their own learning. He realizes the challenges in our current public educational institutions and meets them head-on. His unique blend of educational background, technical expertise, and humor makes him a successful driving force for this change. Hooker also works as a keynote speaker and consultant through his company HookerTech, LLC.

Contents

Preface

In January of 2010, Steve Jobs took the stage at a major Apple event to announce the creation of a device that was in between a laptop and a smartphone. When he announced the iPad, the reviews were mixed. Wasn't this something that had been tried before, even with Apple's MessagePad (http://en.wikipedia.org/wiki/MessagePad)? How was this going to work in mainstream society when it was bigger and bulkier than a phone and didn't have the keyboard of a laptop?

At the time of the announcement, I was a virtualization coordinator for the district. The technology director (my boss at the time) looked at me with wonder when I got excited over this announcement. I told him that this is going to change the face of education. In response he said, "I bet they don't sell even a million of them. It's like a crappy version of a laptop, only you can only do one thing at a time on it. It doesn't even have a USB port!"

In retrospect, I should have taken that bet, as Apple would go on to sell a million in preorder sales alone. Flash forward a few more months. On April 2nd, I was promoted to the role of director of instructional technology. The next day, the first-generation iPad began to be sold in U.S. stores. I point this all out to say that even with all the prep work and sweat necessary for a successful device deployment, some synergy is also required.

As director of instructional technology, I was taking over a dying role of sorts. Many districts were cutting the position at that time in Texas, and some felt it was a "nice to have" more than "a need to have" position. Knowing that going in, I made it one of my personal missions to erase the thought in the minds of the purse-string holders that my position could ever be seen as obsolete. In fact, I set out to do the exact opposite: make them believe they couldn't function successfully without it.

A big part of any leadership position is assessing risks. With the announcement of the iPad, my mind immediately went to education. How could these devices help students personalize their own learning? How would they enhance students' engagement and their learning experience? Are those gains in engagement and personalization enough to justify giving every student one of these devices?

These questions plus many others went through my mind and those of many of the leaders in my district in the months to come. Ultimately, we tried a small pilot of six iPads at the Westlake High School library to see what students and teachers thought. They were extremely well received, but with a bond just failing in the fall of 2010, there didn't seem to be much hope of ever getting more of them into the hands of students.

Enter the second synergistic event. A group of leaders including myself made a trip to Cupertino, California, for an executive briefing on Apple's thoughts on iPads in education. Before lunch on the first day, the Westlake High School principal leaned over and said to us, "We need one of these for every student." At that time, iPads were considered purely consumptive devices—a nice way to read a book or take notes, but offering nothing in the way of creation. That trip to Apple's headquarters changed all of that for skeptics in the room.

When we returned, we went on to expand the pilot to about 70 different users. From special education students to principals to high school AP teachers, we had as many key stakeholders as possible get their hands on this device to put it through its paces. At this point the iPad2 had just launched and had a lot more functionality on the creation end than its predecessor, namely the addition of a camera.

The pilot would go on to expand into Westlake High School the following fall and eventually expand to all 8,000 K–12 Eanes ISD students by the spring of 2013. Here's an early blog post right after launch of the pilot on the Eanes WIFI site: http://tinyurl.com/oez2now. Along the way, I've seen the highs and lows of having a device for every student, especially one as nimble and easy-to-use as an iPad.

The Mobile Learning Mindset series chronicles that journey in terms of six different components. Each component was key to making the initiative as successful as it's become, and as you'll learn, they are all intertwined with each other. This series is not specifically geared toward a 1:1 or Bring Your Own Device (BYOD) initiative. It's meant to be read as a hands-on guide for any teacher, leader, or parent who is involved with a school that is using mobile device technology in the classroom.

The first book went into detail about what district leadership can and should do to make a mobile device initiative successful. Having a strong, clearly defined, and well-communicated goal and vision for a district is an important part of the process. From the superintendent, to the school board, to the district- and campus-level administrators, all need to be singing the same lyrics in the song of 1:1, or else it may fall flat.

The second book in the series is specifically focused on campus leaders and how they can support and showcase the initiative at the campus level. That book focused on the role the campus leader plays in terms of parent communication, teacher expectations, and highlighting student-led projects in the classroom.

This book, the third in the series, is focused on diving into ideas and best practices for professional development around a 1:1 initiative. I've seen many a district, including my own, continue the previous practices of professional development, a "sit 'n' get" style of learning, all the while preaching about how the students need to be the center of the learning. This book focuses on how to make that shift in your organization and offers ideas on how to make learning more engaging for your staff.

Book four is an in-depth look at how mobile devices affect the classroom and what teachers can do both right out of the box and further down the road to sustain a successful student-led learning environment. Using mobile devices just as a substitute for a textbook is a waste of money. These devices are multimedia studios of creation, but many times that use is restricted by the classroom teacher. This book uses models such as SAMR and TPACK to shift the way the learning takes place from a traditional classroom to a mobile classroom.

One major part of a mobile learning initiative is keeping community parents educated on the ins and outs of having mobile devices around the home. This is the focus of the fifth book. Part of the disruptive shift that mobile devices have on learning also affects the home. Parents are now facing dilemmas involving social media, cyberbullying, and digital footprints that their parents never had to deal with. This book will serve as an instruction manual of sorts for parents raising kids in the digital age.

None of this is possible without proper technical support. From infrastructure to break-fix scenarios, having a technology services department on board is vital. The final book in the series is centered around that support. Technology changes so frequently that it is nearly impossible to create a book that has all the latest trends and gadgets. This book will focus on some necessary components of supporting a 1:1 mobile device initiative, as well as how to work with leaders, teachers, trainers, and parents on making the initiative a success.

Each book follows a similar format. Included among the chapters will be "Top 10 Things *Not* to Do," an interview with an expert in that book's particular focus area, and chapters dedicated to ideas and strategies for interacting with all the other "players" in a mobile device initiative. In other words, how does a district leader support their teachers in this new environment? What expectations should the campus administrator have for their staff in terms of professional development? And conversely, how can professional development support those expectations?

All six of these components are parts of the complex, constantly evolving machine that is a mobile learning initiative. Each plays its part, and each requires different amounts of attention and support from the other parts in order to work efficiently. Neglecting one of these components will result in the other parts having to work harder and could ultimately cause the machine to break down. My hope is that if you use this book series to learn how all the parts work, your own mobile learning machine will be a thing of beauty for your students. After all, their learning and their future is the ultimate reason to do something as bold as carrying out an initiative to use mobile devices in the classroom.

Good luck, and thank you for being a part of this mobile learning revolution!

—Carl Hooker

INTRODUCTION

"A Gift with a Tail"

No, I'm not describing a new puppy (although that would apply as well), but instead the feeling districts get when they purchase new technology. Since many school districts fund technology initiatives with a capital bond project or referendum, there are often limits on what those funds can be used for. Districts can buy 20,000 brand new netbooks, but there are no funds allocated to implementation or integration of the devices.

When we first started down the road of our L.E.A.P. initiative (then called the "Westlake Initiative For Innovation" or WIFI Project), our state had recently reduced the amount of funds allocated for public schools. While we didn't lose any teachers due to these cuts, it did mean losing more than half of the staff we had in place for technology integration. So on the heels of launching our first-ever one-to-one pilot, we now had to figure out how to help teachers with the integration of a mobile device in their classroom with less support than they were used to. Add to that the reduction of their extra planning period, and we were forced to commit two cardinal sins: removing support and reducing time.

Anytime you commit funds to an initiative, you must make sure you have both a culture that believes in it (see the first two books in this series) and the support and training to make the change happen.

How to Use This Book

This book is broken into various chapters that will serve as both a guide and a resource at times during various stages of your mobile learning initiative. The structure of the chapters in this book mirrors the structure of the other books in the series, though the content differs.

If the first two books really tackle the why, the first chapter is all about what comes after that—the "How." Part of that how is belief in the "why," but there are ways in which the "how" can encompass the "why." We'll also talk a little bit about the timing of staff development around mobile devices in the first chapter.

The second chapter is dedicated to the ways *not* to run a mobile device initiative when it comes to professional development. Timing, discussion around classroom management, and expectations are a big part of things *not* to forget or address. This chapter really begins to outline many of the other chapters throughout the book when it comes to delivery and content of professional learning.

Chapter 3 is an interview with Educational Technology trainer and consultant Kathy Schrock. Kathy has been a librarian, a technology director, and even a preserver of historical microfilm. She works with districts all over the world with both the initial training and the taking of deeper dives into mobile learning. I've had the pleasure of seeing Kathy present at multiple places and always walk away inspired with something new.

The middle chapters focus on both the people and the expectations around growth and professional learning. Humans have a limited capacity for learning new things, and force-feeding mobile learning to them can actually be detrimental to a program. Learning should be designed around their current knowledge, with examples of how mobile devices can help make learning more interactive and engaging for students.

In Chapters 6 and 7, we'll look at ways to find opportunities for learning besides just the summertime. Think about where you learn. Is it sitting at a desk in your office? Or is it at a coffee shop or comfortable couch at home? Professional learning for adults is usually limited to uncomfortable spaces (like those hard wooden library chairs) and delivered at times when teachers' brains are either exhausted (at the end of the year) or distracted (at the beginning of the year). We'll also investigate how we can leverage our own amazing teachers to showcase and share best practices. Learning a new mobile tool is a good excuse to tear down the silos in classrooms and create a community of learning around the same goal.

Chapter 8 is an overview of my favorite professional learning concept around mobile devices, called Interactive Learning Challenges (ILCs). These challenges (also known as the APPMazing Race in some circles) highlight a new way of learning that mobile devices enable. Staff participate in collaborative teams to complete a series of interactive challenges using their mobile devices to create learning artifacts. This is done to encourage movement and also highlight the fact that learning can take place in places other than the classroom desk.

In our final two chapters, we tie together the other components of this book series and how they interact with professional learning. Teachers obviously need to see the value in professional learning, but they also need to be valued for what they learn and share. District and campus leaders need to create environments where adults are celebrated for their learning. The technology department has to support this professional learning by providing devices quickly to staff and also making sure that all the necessary components, such as wireless, are in working order. Finally, parents also need to see the value in funding support for professional learning and the time that is needed to make sure it's effective. Professional learning directly affects the learning of their students.

Brain Breaks

Movement is a central theme throughout this book series, but especially when it comes to mobile learning. Why have mobile devices that you can capture and create on when you are tied to a desk? Throughout this book, I've placed some ideas for brain breaks in professional learning. These are in separate boxes and embedded in different parts of the chapters. While there are many more than the ones I share, I've placed some of my favorites in this book. I hope you can use them in your next professional development activity.

"Easter Eggs"

According to Wikipedia, an Easter egg is "an inside joke, hidden message, or feature in an interactive work such as a computer program, video game, or DVD menu screen." Why can't we also have these in books? In this book, I've hidden several Easter eggs that you'll have to uncover and discover. I've buried some in words, others in images. How do you reveal them? If you are reading this book in its paper form, you'll need to download the Aurasma app (www.aurasma.com/#/whats-your-aura) and find the trigger images to unlock the Easter eggs. Find and follow the "MLM Lead" channel to make it all work. Instructions can be found here: http://mrhook.it/eggs. Happy hunting!

AFTER THE "WHY" COMES THE "HOW"

In Simon Sinek's TED Talk on "How great leaders inspire action" (http://mrhook.it/sinek) he discusses what he calls the "Golden Circle" of what makes certain people or companies successful. The root of his talk (and later his first book) is that as leaders we must always focus our attention on the "Why" whenever starting a project or initiative.

While a majority of his talk and book center around this leadership concept of "why," the "how" is really where the rubber meets the road. In a mobile device initiative, that "how" is almost directly attributable to professional learning and support. Staff can have complete belief in the concept of personalized learning with mobile devices (the "why"), but without a way to implement, train, model, and share (the "how"), most initiatives will struggle or fail.

Investigating the Effect of the "How"

I had the pleasure of working with a district recently on this concept of "how." For the sake of this story I'll call them South Texas ISD (a fictional district). South Texas had a great leader who really was a believer in using mobile devices for learning. He shared his vision with the staff and community and eventually got funds through a bond to supply all 25,000 of his students.

Everyone was on board with the "why," but when it came time to implement, there was a problem: They only had a small amount of funds to pay for support and training staff. Although the initial deployment had help from the company that supplied the devices, there were very few support personnel. It just so happens that this district began its mobile device initiative the same year we began ours at Eanes ISD. So when I went to visit them four years later, not knowing their support history, I assumed they would be in much the same place as our district.

To my surprise, the staff of South Texas ISD were still struggling with integration, and much of the staff were still on the substitution level of Dr. Ruben Puentedura's SAMR model (http://hippasus.com/rrpweblog/). How could this be possible? I probed their Director of Instructional Technology a bit and discovered that they had one support person for every 8,000 devices. Compare that with my district, which handed out 8,000 student devices and has 10 instructional support staff on hand. This made me wonder if the same was true for other districts that had higher levels versus lower levels of support. Would those with more support and training be much more successful on their integration? What follows are the results of that research, which really showcases the importance of the "how" to make the "why" successful.

INSTRUCTIONAL TECHNOLOGY SUPPORT SURVEY

Date of the Survey: Fall 2014

Participating District Data

There were 28 districts participating in the survey, primarily from Texas. Of those, the largest had a student enrollment of 45,000 and the smallest had just 362 students. Twelve of the 28 districts surveyed (43%) had a 1:1 program on one or more of their campuses. There was a combined student enrollment of 256,000 students, with more than 210,000 devices being supported.

Participating District Data

There were 28 districts participating in the survey, primarily from Texas. Of those, the largest had a student enrollment of 45,000 and the smallest had just 362 students. Twelve of the 28 districts surveyed (43%) had a 1:1 program on one or more of their campuses. There was a combined student enrollment of 256,000 students, with more than 210,000 devices being supported.

Who Filled Out the Survey

The majority of those responding to the survey were technology directors, CTOs, or instructional technology coordinators. I recognize there can be a level of bias when it comes to evaluating your own level of support or integration, but I found their answers to be extremely realistic, and the outliers tended to cancel each other out. In fact, taking that bias inflation out of the results actually gives the findings even more impact in some ways.

Staffing Ratios

In general, districts fund two technology support technicians for every one of their instructional technology specialists. As the survey data revealed, this has a direct impact on how well districts are supporting technology (most respondents felt they did a strong job of supporting technology) to how well they are integrating it (most felt they did a weak or adequate job of integration).

Outcomes

A majority of districts (69%) surveyed felt they had adequate to excellent level of support for technology. By contrast, only 41% of districts felt they were integrating technology at least adequately, with only one stating they were doing an excellent job integrating technology.

Those districts that scored the highest on integration of technology into classroom and curriculum had either one full-time staff member on a campus dedicated to that role or a full-time staff member who served multiple campuses. Those with only one full-time district person to support the entire district or no person dedicated to this role scored the lowest.

Almost all (96%) stated that turnaround time on a technology work order was expected to be 5 days or less.

Only 28% of districts surveyed felt that they had "Strong" or "Exceptional" professional development around the area of technology integration on their campuses. Those campuses that rated high in professional development also had more staff members dedicated to integration of technology.

Conclusion

More people equals better support and integration of technology. Although that seems like a no-brainer, digging into the data revealed a level of disparity between "support" and "integration" in these districts. The ratio of technicians (1 per 999 students) versus that of instructional technology specialists (1 per 1910 students) seems to be the highest contributing factor to this. If the technology doesn't work, then you can't integrate it. That seems to be the mantra districts are following with these staffing ratios (we follow a similar ratio at Eanes ISD). However, if districts truly want to use these tools for learning, it would appear the next step is figuring out a way to fund that professional support person to help integrate the technology, whether at one campus (ideally) or at multiple campuses. A summary of this data is given in an infographic located on my website: http://mrhook.it/ratio

What Does This Mean for Professional Learning?

If a mobile device initiative were a car, the teachers would most certainly be the drivers. The district leaders would be the bank that ultimately chooses the car (device) and finances it. The campus leader is the GPS that gives the car direction, and the classroom is the road. Technology departments provide the maintenance and upkeep as well as fix any flat tires or cracked windshields.

In this scenario, professional learning is most certainly the gas that makes the car go. You can have everyone on board and loaded into the car with a clear path, but without a way to put things in motion, the learning sits idle. As you read through the chapters in this book and begin to discover ideas for moving the car forward, always be thinking about the parts necessary to move the initiative forward.

BRAIN BREAK

Giant Rochambeau

Materials Needed: None

Concept: A quick way to create mutual support through friendly competition

Audience Size: 20–500

Set-up: The childhood game rock-paper-scissors is something that everyone can relate to. In this version, everyone finds an initial partner and plays the game. (Note: Be sure to clearly define when you should "throw" your rock, paper, or scissors.) If you beat someone, they become your cheerleader, and you go on to face someone else (and their cheerleader). If you beat them, they join your cheering section. Eventually the game will continue until you have two people left with half the audience cheering for one person and the other group cheering for the other.

CHAPTER 2

TOP 10 THINGS *NOT* TO DO

As I mentioned in the introduction to this book, we committed a couple of cardinal sins when instituting a new initiative. We cut back teachers' extra planning time and reduced the number of support positions on campuses. These were short-sighted changes made in an attempt to save budgetary dollars, but they were detrimental to the advancement of staff learning with these new devices.

While we would eventually overcome those mistakes and reinstitute the Educational Technology position as well as adding in a planning period, we still made plenty of other mistakes when it came to training staff in a 1:1 environment. It is through those mistakes that we have generated this list. So, when embarking on your own device initiative, be sure to heed the warnings listed here, or you might consider returning this gift with a tail.

1. Do *Not* Wait until the Last Minute to Give the Devices to Staff

Because of the timing of our bond package and when funds could become available, we didn't actually have iPads in hand and branded until mid-July. That meant many teachers only had the iPads in their hands for a month or less. As a result, many teachers did not have time to even think about how *they* would use the device, much less what their students would do with them.

Technology may be prevalent in the real world, but in the classroom, it's still a relatively new concept when it comes to teaching and learning, especially with mobile devices. Teachers trying to implement mobile devices in their classroom need time to plan, prepare, and really become comfortable with the concept of the disruption this technology poses. A great deal of that comfort comes from experience. We recommend having a device like the students' in the hands of teachers at least 6 months before implementation.

While our ultimate goal is for the pedagogy to shift from teacher-centered to student-led, teachers need to be familiar with the variables technology can introduce before they give up some level of control of their classroom to the students.

2. Do *Not* Forget to Address Classroom Management

As stated earlier, the concept of the traditional classroom and teacher control is completely disrupted when you introduce a mobile device for every student. The beauty and educational relevance of these devices is the personalization of learning that can happen. The level of personalization that can happen in a classroom is directly attributed to the style in which learning takes place.

While personalization is the ultimate goal, there are steps that need to happen to transition from the traditional non-device model to the more dynamic, student-led mobile learning model. Part of that transition happens in the realm of classroom management. I've been in classrooms with extremely strict rules for use of the devices. These classrooms are commonly the same ones that gravitate toward more of a lecture-style approach to teaching. These students now have the power of the world at their fingertips, yet teachers still feel the need to shut them down for entire 50-minute class periods.

Tight control over where information comes from can be a giant hindrance in the advancement of your device program. As I toured traditional classrooms when we first started our initiative, it wasn't uncommon to see all the students sitting in their rows, watching the teacher with their devices face-up. On occasion, though, I would notice a kid using their iPad as some sort of steering wheel. I discovered later that the game *Temple Run* was gaining in popularity, and it was much more interesting than information the teacher at the front of them room was lecturing about.

Classroom environments that have the best management techniques tend to be much more student-centered. In other words, there are times when technology isn't used but the students are still owning their learning through discussion and collaboration. The technology almost becomes invisible because the students are given an assignment to work and collaborate on, and the thought of playing *Temple Run* never enters their minds. They are now an active part of the classroom, and the learning objective is their goal, so they no longer feel the need to check out mentally.

3. Do *Not* Expect Technology to Be Used All the Time at the Highest Level

I have long been preaching the SAMR model by Dr. Ruben Puentedura as the way teaching should progress in a 1:1 (or any) environment. While his model hits home in many ways, I always struggle with the concept of SAMR as a "ladder." I once had a teacher text me to tell me he had reached Redefinition and as a result was "all done" with technology integration. This idea that redefinition is our goal with everything in the class has always bothered me.

I was inspired by my colleague Greg Garner (@classroom_tech on Twitter) and his analogy of what teaching and learning with technology is like. He felt, and I agreed, that the ladder analogy should be transformed into something much more fluid … like a swimming pool. And so, the "SAMR Swimming Pool"

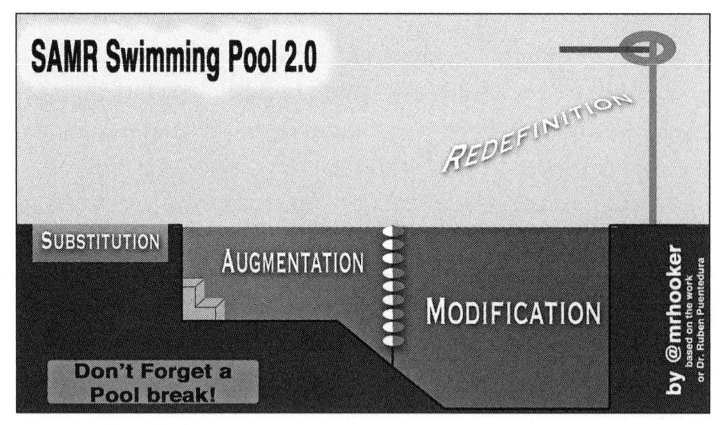

Figure 2.1 The SAMR swimming pool analogy was an idea that originated with Greg Garner's take on Dr. Rubin Puentedura's SAMR ladder.

Within this analogy, teachers can shift between the shallow and deep end of the pool when using technology with their students. They may even find a time to take a "pool break" and have no technology used for a certain collaborative project.

The bottom line is, when you are training teachers on the use of technology, you need to emphasize that technology can be used in many different ways but doesn't necessarily need to be on all day. In fact, for the struggling teacher it might be better to start in the shallow end of the pool (Substitution and Augmentation) rather than just jumping right into the deep end.

4. Do *Not* Limit Staff Training to the Summer

As I mentioned at the beginning of the chapter, because of budgetary cuts our high school teachers lost an extra planning period that was considered "PLC time." This time was framed around Dufour's Professional Learning Communities model and allowed for same-subject-area teachers to have a common planning time to grow and learn. On top of that, as mentioned, we cut back our educational technologists across the district. Both of these factors could have killed the program and definitely kept us from transforming teaching and learning as much as we would have liked. Research points out that teachers will ultimately determine the success of the program, so it's worth investing in them. model was born.

The problem with traditional K–12 public institutions is that the majority of staff training happens during the summer months. The research of Robert Marzano and the findings in Project Red talk about how one of the key traits to successful implementation of 1:1 is monthly training, led at minimum by the principal and key leaders to give teachers the tools they need. Ideally time is set aside daily for this discussion, as in the PLC model, but at the very least holding weekly "Lunch & Learns" or monthly "Appy Hours" are methods of getting teachers to meet regularly to discuss tools and strategies throughout the year.

The summer may be the only "obvious" time available for teacher learning, but some districts are becoming more creative by implementing teacher prep days or late start/early release days throughout the year. This allows teachers time to reflect, adjust, and plan more lessons around mobile devices rather than just a "drive-by" training over one day in the summer. While the summer may be the primary opportunity for some districts, don't waste that time having teachers sit and listen when they are now mobile—which leads to my next point.

5. Do *Not* Forget to Model How You Want Them to Teach

As stated in the classroom management section, the most powerful and effective use of mobile devices in the classroom comes when they are allowed to be mobile. However, when we train teachers, we forget that this is the case so we lock them into desks or round tables and make them sit and listen about how they shouldn't make their students just sit and listen.

The motto "Don't be the sage on the stage, be the guide on the side" has been worn out in education. I like the phrase "mentor in the center" or, as Discovery Education Primary Consultant Dean Shareski (http://twitter.com/shareski) calls it, "the meddler in the middle." In the mobile classroom, the teacher's role is to harness the chaotic energy flowing in and out of the devices and direct it toward some sort of learning objective.

Our training should model this exact behavior. Although there is a time to go over some instructions, the teachers being trained should be doing more of the heavy lifting than the presenter. (More about this in Point 9.) If you believe at all in the "Learning Pyramid" model, then you realize that lecture only counts for about 5% memory retention, whereas actually doing (or teaching) a concept equates to 75% to 90% retention.

6. Do *Not* Forget to Cover the Basics of Digital Workflow

The old days of file structures and local drives are over. With the proliferation of mobile devices, files exist on the device or, more likely, in the cloud. In order to get materials to and from students, there needs to be some solution in place for this.

Starting at the substitutive level, this means a way for a teacher to hand out a PDF (instead of a worksheet), have the student annotate it, then turn it back in digitally. One of our biggest gaffes early on is that we didn't have a solution in place when we started our pilot. Email ended up being the best and really only way we could get files back and forth on our iPads.

Teachers with more than 150 students quickly felt their brains sinking under the weight of an overloaded inbox. We ended up going with a Content Management System (CMS) that would help them with workflow of items on that substitutive level as a way to bridge the gap between their analog world of the past and the new digital one they were entering.

The good news is, with more and more applications becoming web-based, it's only a matter of time until the only thing a student will be turning in is a URL that goes to all of their posted work. And with Google and Apple becoming big

BRAIN BREAK

Idea Toss

Materials Needed: Pieces of paper in any size

Concept: A way to quickly share ideas around a question or a problem.

Audience Size: 10+

Set-up: Pose a question or wondering to the group. Have each participant write down their idea on a sheet or small piece of paper and then crumple it into a ball. Once everyone has crumpled their ideas, count down from 3 and have everyone toss their idea across the room. Then they find a new "idea" from someone else and find a partner to share ideas they discovered.

Example: What is something you would like to change about your classroom environment? Participants might write down: "More color on the walls" or "Flexible furniture" and then toss their idea.

(free) players in the CMS space with Classroom and iTunes U, respectively, districts embarking on a 1:1 today will have many more options than we did back in 2011.

7. Do *Not* Focus on the Apps During Training

We've all had an app so cool, so inspiring, we just had to share with everyone else how great it was. As with anything in the tech world, change happens quickly. With apps, it is even faster. So armed with that knowledge, it would make sense to avoid spending too much time on very specific apps. Instead, let the focus of training be on pedagogy and how the technology can make the curriculum come to life.

In classrooms where this concept works really well, as I've said before, the technology is almost invisible. Instead of being a lesson around the Explain Everything app or Google Spreadsheets, it's a lesson around using various technology tools to show your learning. Although part of that process can be important, and knowing the tools available helps, we tend to design our professional learning backwards. Instead of focusing how we should change our pedagogy to better leverage technology, we focus more on how to make an app work with the hopes that the teacher will come up with an idea for integration. Keep the focus on those learning objectives, and the apps will begin to naturally make an appearance.

8. Do *Not* Make All Required Training Face-to-Face

We live in a world where content (especially entertainment) is on-demand and available at any time. We no longer have to buy an entire album; we can download one song. We don't have to wait until Thursday night at 8 p.m. to catch our favorite *Friends* episode (ok, that's a dated reference); it's available on

Netflix or captured via DVR. Despite all of these advances, we still teach on a schedule-heavy, all or nothing basis. Advances in blended learning and flipped instruction allow for some of that learning to be flexible for students, but in the area of professional learning, the focus is still primarily on seat-time.

Some fellow administrators have asked me, "How do you know they are learning if they aren't in the room?" My response: "How do you know they are learning if they *are* in the room?" I've sat in many an inservice as a teacher and watched as colleagues surfed their Facebook feeds, shopped for ideas on Pinterest, or, even more overtly, sat and graded papers. What does that say about the face-to-face learning? The attendees are choosing to do something else other than listen to the presenter.

When it comes to online options for professional learning, it's been a virtual wasteland. Districts either purchase subscription-based video tutorials or promote webinars that are actually worse than face-to-face because you can't even tell if people are paying attention (here's a hint: they aren't). However, there is a bit of a movement being made to take some of the same traits of blended learning and bring them to the professional learning world. Tools such as Swivl and easy, free online module creators like Moodle and iTunes U mean that learning tasks can be captured and put online for preview or review. Furthermore, using online collaboration through tools like Google Community and Edmodo means that a group that does meet face-to-face once can continue the conversation throughout the year online.

9. Do *Not* Make the Training All About One Person

Just as in Point 5, we need to make sure the training we are providing isn't focused on a single instructor. Learning happens in all sorts of ways, and having one person talk at you for 6 hours usually isn't the most optimal way to use a teacher's time. As mentioned in Point 8, teachers will selectively "opt out" of learning by focusing on other tasks if given the option of listening to a person talk for more than 20 minutes.

We are faced with such a time famine that teachers crave time to collaborate and socialize with each other during professional learning sessions. David Weinberger says the smartest person in the room is the room (Weinberger, 2012), so why not take advantage of that social energy and weaponize it for learning?

Professional learning that shifts the focus to the "student" can be powerful, but that means you need to go beyond giving them meaningless tasks to accomplish in isolation. With every adult in the room having one (or more) mobile devices, it's time to take advantage of this new mobile world when it comes to learning.

One of the most effective methods of professional learning I've ever used is something I call "Interactive Learning Challenges" or "The APPMazing Race." You'll read more about these in a later chapter, but the gist is that learning happens collectively and collaboratively. Giving teachers a series of challenges to complete while moving around the room and even outside of the room activates all sorts of new learning conversations. But most importantly, it makes the training about more than just the person standing at the front of the room.

10. Do *Not* Ignore the Impact of Campus Leadership's Role in Professional Learning

A campus principal can either accelerate or destroy an initiative before it gets off the ground. Dr. Anthony Muhammad says that the person of most importance in a district when it comes to making change happen is the campus leader. The campus principal should be seen as the master of instruction in a building, but too often they are dealing with HR issues or PR problems. The principal's role as instructional leader diminishes more and more until, eventually, they don't even pursue their own professional learning.

It's imperative for any district starting down the path of mobile learning that campus leadership be a part of the process, including the professional learning.

One of the most amazing workshops I've ever given was recently in McAllen, TX. This is a district that started their 1:1 program the same year we did, but they had more devices than us by fourfold. I was asked to come in and put together a series of Interactive Learning Challenges to really open up staff to the power of mobile devices in their classrooms. It wasn't unlike many trainings I had given to my own staff or other workshops and conferences around the county. However, this event had one major difference. The 75 staff members in attendance were all joined by their campus principals in the learning experience. And as I surveyed the room throughout the day, I was floored to see their superintendent Dr. Ponce working as part of a group during one of the APPmazing Race challenges. He had been there the entire day learning alongside all of his staff.

That kind of leadership is invaluable for any initiative, but especially when it comes to modeling the behavior principals are asking their teachers to adopt. These principals not only realize the value of the "gift" of mobile devices in the classroom; they also realize the necessity of the "tail" that comes along with that gift. With their support and ownership, the initiative might stumble at times—but it will *not* fail.

CHAPTER 3

INTERVIEW WITH KATHY SCHROCK

Kathy Schrock is a professional learning expert and someone I would truly call a "lifelong learner." A former librarian, she presents at educational technology conferences all over the globe and is credited with many different strategies and concepts in learning with mobile devices. One of my favorite is her Bloomin' Apps posts integrating Bloom's Taxonomy with a variety of apps to use for learning (http://mrhook.it/bloom).

Kathy Schrock

When writing a book about professional learning, I could think of no one better to talk about adult learning than Kathy. I've had the pleasure of watching her present multiple concepts to a wide range of audiences, and I always leave one of her sessions inspired and eager to apply what I learned. What follows is my interview with Kathy and some of the concepts she uses when creating a productive and exciting environment for adults to learn in. (*Note:* Go to http://mrhook.it/schrock to see the full interview online.)

Carl Hooker (CH): As this particular book focuses on professional learning, I'm very excited to have the guru, the queen of all things PD, Kathy Schrock, join us.

Kathy Schrock (KS): Thank you, Carl—I hope I can live up to your expectations.

CH: *(Laughing)* You already have! If nothing else, you have a beautiful lighthouse behind you there.

KS: There you go.

CH: Before we get started, tell me a little bit about yourself. What's your origin story in education and made you who you are today?

KS: Well, I was one of those people that always sat on the first row. Someone who some of the educational humorists call a "bow head"—you know, with the little bow on my head, always raising my hand. I just loved school. So I knew very early on what I wanted to do was teach, because my elementary teachers were, you know, varied in their approach but definitely inspired me at the same time. So that's why I decided to become an educator.

CH: What kind of educational positions have you held over the years?

KS: So I've been in the public sector somewhat, too. I've been a public librarian, an historical librarian, an historical microfilmer. I actually got to do all of Thomas Nast's original works in the Montgomery Ward catalog.

CH: *(Laughs)*

KS: Just something to do on the side. It was preservation microfilming, so it was a pretty big deal. I've been a school librarian in a middle school, I've been a high school librarian and a community college librarian. Then when all the tech stuff came in, I was primarily self-taught. and I started doing all the tech stuff, so I became the Technology Director of a school district by default because I knew more than anybody else (about technology), and then another [tech director position], and then retired from school districts in 2011.

CH: Wow! So a lot of curation of knowledge there with the library background, and then very self-taught when it comes to the tech stuff. So with all that knowledge, kind of go back in time and, you mentioned microfilm, but maybe go back and tell me what your earliest experience with what we now call "ed tech" was in schools.

KS: The earliest I ever remember using was a Tachistoscope in 6th grade....

CH: I'm sorry, what? Can you say that again?

KS: *(Laughs)* A Tachistoscope. What it would do was highlight words in a frame and it would go faster and faster to help you read. But I just loved it because it really increased my reading speed and comprehension. I just loved it. And that was in 6th grade, but let's fast forward to 1983 when I was the fill-in librarian at a high school and I used reel-to-reel tape to create an introduction to the library. You can see that on my Vimeo page (video here: https://vimeo.com/126691756) I have long bushy hair, and I'm really young. The students in it would just hate watching it, and I even used copyrighted music in it because you know, at the time, what did I know? Nothing. "Sure! It's a Police song that's popular! We'll use that!"

CH: That's funny—when I was teaching first grade I did the same thing. I used a totally copyrighted song by this band called Blur from the U.K. I remember my kids got really into it, and thinking to myself, "If that ever made it onto the web, I'd be in big trouble."

KS: *(Laughs)* Exactly!

CH: We learn as we go, I guess. So, I've seen you train and present several times, and you've probably trained people from all over the world. One thing that I've discovered over the years is that when you go to a session or you present a session, there may be that one person who may not be that into what you are teaching or isn't that on board with it. What do you do with that person that isn't really on board with what you are teaching, or get them to learn to turn them around?

KS: Well, in whole group, I try not to train more than 50 people in a hands-on workshop at a time. So once I get everyone working and I see a person "checked out" or leaning back because we're in a small group, I try to differentiate. I go over and talk to them and try to find something that they are interested in. Whatever the project, just target something different for them.

Recently I did a secondary workshop for a school district in Alabama. There was a whole of group of people, and they were interested, but they really weren't doing the project. So I sort of sidled over there, and it turns out they were all coaches. They were teachers, but they were also coaches. So once I showed them the "Coach's Eye" app from Tech Smith, they were all "Can we use this?!" So you have to know enough about the apps so you can find something that interests them. As a librarian, it's not that uncommon, because you know pretty much all the content. So, just find something that was interesting for them. What I wanted them to do, or what they were supposed to be doing, was using the iPad to find out ways to support teaching and learning, and for them, that's exactly what they wanted.

So you just differentiate. Which isn't that hard, but with more than 50 people that can become difficult.

CH: That's funny, because that's what we always tell our teachers to do—differentiate—in their classes, but then when they go to PD, what do they get? It's kind of the standard, canned professional development. That's awesome that you do that, and smart that you keep your group sizes small. Think about class sizes of 35 or so students—imagine differentiating with 50 to 100 educators in a room.

KS: Right. They act just like their students, so it's OK. *(Laughs)* You know, you can tell which grade a person teaches just by looking at them sometimes. It's pretty funny.

CH: What's the difference between teaching adults and teaching kids?

KS: The real difference is you can't really be sarcastic with kids and can't tell jokes. You have to be really careful about what you present. Although with adults, sometimes, it kind of depends on where you are. Some of my northeastern, New England, born-in-New-Jersey-style doesn't go over so well in other countries or places, so you pretty much have to keep everything sort of neutral as far as that stuff goes. But they can also be the same. If they are an elementary teacher, they are very used to things being organized and step-by-step. Not that they are all concrete-sequential like I am, but they might rather have it that way for them. Then you have other people that have different types of classes, might not be so structured, whatever grade they are, and they just are like, "Give me the project and I'll figure it out on my own." So you just have to be prepared to wear many different hats.

CH: Yeah, I've learned over the years that you have to differentiate a little bit. So some people can speed ahead if they want to, as you said, but I know a lot of teachers who also like the "1, 2, 3, 4" style of training.

KS: Right.

CH: What's one of your favorite topics right now that you like to train on? Is there something right now that you really love talking about with educators?

KS: Well what I like to do a lot of, and what I love is—you know a lot of schools bought a lot of devices, and they know how to use them but they aren't sure how to use them with students. How to help students create for assessment. So consumption is not a problem, but creation is. And that's something that goes from administrators all the way down. So I did an administrator workshop the other day, with 50 in the morning and 50 in the afternoon, and all they used was Explain Everything. I figured for them, one app in depth was a good thing to focus on and use.

With educators I use apps that are subject neutral so the projects are based on their passion. Or if they are in a group, it's what the group decides. What the consensus is. Sometimes if I'm trying to introduce an app, I do something on measurement where they have a screen shot it and drop it into Explain Everything and explain area and perimeter, which freaks people out that haven't done area and perimeter in a long time.

CH: *(Laughs)*

KS: But there is a little help file, and there are always people in the group who can do it. But most of the time I try and stay away from the content. I just give them the structure, and they can create the project on whatever content they want. That's what I like to do. The more you leave it open, the more everyone's creativity comes out.

CH: Yeah, you give them some ideas, you know, like give a little nudge to those that are just staring at a blank screen while others can just fly with it.

KS: Right, and I usually have people in pairs. And I try to mix them up so it's not the person they came with but it's someone else. That usually works out well, especially if someone has a dead device or if someone forgot their device. That works really well.

CH: Which is good modeling for schools, because that will happen all the time where little Johnny forgot to charge his device.

KS: Exactly.

CH: So you mentioned you let them create off of their passions. When it comes to your passions, where do you go for inspiration or to create these ideas? Since you are out there a lot, what are some things you see out there that inspire you?

KS: I usually go to workshops or presentations on things that I don't know anything about. I'll listen. And then if there's another session on that same thing I'll go to that, too. I'll then decide if it's something that I want to put my passion into. And if it is, I'll think about how it can support teaching and learning in a meaningful way, I'll create a webpage about it, I'll create a presentation. I might not create an entire workshop about it, because I might not want to go that in-depth or invest myself into it when there are people out there where that's their lifelong passion and they can do it better than I can.

But I'll get the resources together for teachers who have gone to one of these [sessions] and want more information. They want tutorials. They want sample lessons. Basically, while I'm collecting this information, I'm learning myself.

But there are some things, and don't ask me to name them because I won't, that are noticeably absent from my webpage. There are common trends in education and ed tech that we hear a lot about, but they are not things that I believe truly support teaching and learning, so when people ask me "Why don't you have this?" I'm, well, you know, not really a big fan of "this" and I don't want to just do it halfway. If I don't support it in my heart, then I won't do it. Like "Kathy Schlock's Guide to Everything Except *****".

CH: *(Laughs)* That's funny, because you don't even have to say what they are, but I have an idea because I probably have the same ones popping into my head, too. It's interesting that you go and find things that you are interested in. Almost like a classroom teacher. If you aren't interested in your topic, then your students are going to know you are not interested about it. I love that you find and present on things that you are passionate about so you can bring those to the masses. Like I have a thing about numbered lists. But that's smart—if your heart's not in it, don't do it.

KS: You're right. I love the top 10 list, and then the next day it's something else that would supersede something in the top 10, and it's all for naught.

CH: So you have all of these resources, but what do you do to prepare to give a workshop?

KS: I make exemplars of every project or product that I expect them to do, using the choice of tools that they have. I very rarely show those to them, but they are really what in my mind I visualize I want them to be. They don't see them, but at least then I can help them decide—if they are choosing between the capabilities of a couple of different tools, I can help tell them which ones to use.

That's pretty much what I do. It takes quite a bit of time to do them, since they are content neutral so I have to invent some content to put with them. And sometimes they aren't all great educational content that I put in. It might be something like old-time Knicks basketball or something, which I am passionate about.

CH: I'm sorry. They haven't done too well lately.

KS: *(Laughs)* So for teachers when you want students to create classroom projects and products, you don't necessarily have to know the tool inside and out, but you should create some exemplars. You may not have to show them, but at least then you'll have some ideas about the struggles or problems that may come along.

CH: How do you know when a training or workshop has been successful? Like you walk out and think "Wow, I nailed it!"

KS: For a workshop, it's when they finish their projects or products and share them (usually on a Padlet page), when they are anxious to come up and share what they've done, and they are proud of what they've done and you know you've gotten them excited—that's all I can ask. And when I watch people grow in that 2- or 3-hour time period from not knowing how to do something to feeling that huge feeling of success and the ability to go back and do it.

In one workshop I did, there was half of the middle school in the morning and half in the afternoon, and during lunch the director gave me a call to let me know that a person was already instituting something I taught them and the students were loving it. It can't get any better than that!

CH: That's awesome! You know you've struck a chord when that happens.

KS: That's what gets me excited. I don't care about written evaluations—I want to see that glow in their eyes.

CH: So let's go the opposite direction now. Have you ever attended a session where you felt like it wasn't very effective? Why do think that happens, or what happened to make you feel that way?

KS: I've been to some like this and I've also done some like this and felt they were ineffective.

CH: *(Laughs)*

KS: When you have a 3-hour workshop and people come in, they need to have some content to be on the same page. You have to give them an introduction. My introductions last sometimes 45 minutes, and then we do a project and then talk about the next project. But what I used to do was have the projects interspersed in that 45-minute introduction period. Then all the sudden it would become a 3-hour introduction. I'd talk a bit, then they'd do a project, then I'd talk a bit, then another project. A hands-on workshop should be hands-on. So what would happen is they would drag through the project and I'd have to try and bring them back to the content because I want them to get to the content. So what I've found is the most effective is to do the content first, have the devices off and listen. I'll give examples of what we're going to do and then just do project, showcase, project, showcase. When I do that, it goes so much better. And I've been in ones too where it's a "hands-on" workshop and people are sitting there waiting and they are ready because they brought all their stuff and it's charged, but you're still talking. So they know up front that I'm going to be yapping at the beginning for a while, but after that it's all their time. That's what I think makes it more effective.

CH: So you really set the tone for the day and then get them excited and let them work. I like that. It doesn't cut momentum that way.

KS: Exactly. I have, like, 14 projects for them to do in about 2 hours, too. No one will ever finish that many, but for me, having a choice of 14 projects is helpful for someone when I can see something is boring them or maybe they need to go to the next level. I can adjust and say, "OK, now let's go to project 8. From 1 to 8. And now 2. And then 6." Just depending on what's going on, so it's always good to have a whole bunch in your pocket.

CH: Smart. Your day may be outlined in your head, but you can adjust it based on the group reaction.

KS: Right. Or it's something they've glommed onto and I see that they really want to do it.

CH: Last question before we get to rapid fire. Have you been to any sessions recently that have been inspiring or innovative? Have you seen some given in an innovative way or maybe been inspired by a keynote?

KS: Yes. Last month at Ed Tech Teacher's iPad Summit in Boston, Guy Kawasaki was the keynote. He started out by just putting up "10, 20, 30." And I was like, "What is that?" and he went on to explain that you should only have 10 points in a presentation, 20 minutes in terms of length, and use 30-point font for everything to make sure everybody can see it. Then he went on to do that. Although he said it would be a little longer than 20 minutes because he had to fill the time. But truly, it was pretty cool. So I tried one that way, "10, 20, 30," and I can do it—but it's hard to have just me talk for 20 minutes. And he had very basic slides, hardly any content on the slides. Mostly hand-drawn images, not photos. That gave me the idea to try to use something like that. *(Laughs)* I don't know if I can do that exactly maybe "two 20s" so I can do a 40 minute section.

CH: *(Laughs)* Yeah, maybe you should do "20, 40, 60" instead?

KS: *(Laughs)* Yea, I'll just double it. Exactly!

CH: It reminds me of when he did his iPadpalooza keynote, and it was juxtapositioned with Adam Bellow, who has like 473 slides, and his philosophy is "Slides are free, so why not use them?"

KS: *(Laughs)* Right, and I'm somewhere in between. I usually have around 120 slides for an hour-long presentation. I just talk faster. Since I only have you for an hour, I want to put as much in your brain as I possibly can. That's my goal.

CH: OK, we're going to go rapid-fire James Lipton style—are you ready?

KS: Yup!

CH: What is your favorite word?

KS: Octothorpe.

CH: Now I have to stop so I can ask what is "octothorpe"?

KS: Back when the telephone came out, there was the little star and pound sign. The two gentlemen from Bell Labs who invented that were allowed to name those two things. So even though it was a star they decided to call it the octothorpe. And the reason they did that is because it had 8 points and one of the engineers was heavily into getting Jim Thorpe's medals back to him, so that's why it's called the octothorpe.

CH: Oh wow!

KS: So whenever I get a new phone and they tell me to press "pound" or "star," I tell them, "By the way, I'll want you to use 'octothorpe' for the rest of the day today," and they usually agree.

CH: *(Laughs)* OK. I learned something new today!

KS: There you go.

CH: What is your least favorite word?

KS: Using "Google" as a verb.

CH: If you had to have another profession than the one you have right now, what other profession would you attempt?

KS: Probably engineering. That's what they tried to get me to do before I switched to education. I'm pretty good in math and science.

CH: Name something that is cool in your office.

KS: *(Holds up a red stapler)*

CH: Oh, a *red* stapler!!

KS: From *Office Space* (the movie). I also have a Mod-T 3D printer that came last week, so I've been printing little dice and wine glass charms. I only have pink though. I have a page about 3D printing now and I see how it can support teaching and learning rather than just fun. You just sit there and watch it and watch it.

CH: What's something that hasn't been invented that needs to be invented?

KS: I just want a small battery that lasts like a week so we don't have to spend our lives looking for sockets. The sockets in airports, the ones for vacuum cleaners, are now locked because they can't get to them ever. But I just got the new Smart suitcase, so apparently I can charge my devices six times from my suitcase. So we'll find out next week.

CH: We had a company here try to sell us solar-power backpacks, but the problem is, kids are inside all day.

KS: Right, exactly!

CH: What natural talent do you wish you were gifted with?

KS: It's funny you say creativity. I have zero creativity. I can take things and copy them and make stuff and remix stuff. I can make stuff. I know what creativity means, I just can't do it myself. *(Laughs)*

CH: *(Laughs)* I think you are a remixer. That's what I call it. You see an idea and you remix it and make it better.

KS: Yeah, that's good. OK. Remixer.

CH: Last one. What's your favorite motto or expression that you like to live by?

KS: It's from "All Star" by Smash Mouth, and it's "Only shooting stars break the mold."

CH: Perfect. Any final advice?

KS: When giving PD, keep the content neutral, because teachers are much more likely to stretch themselves when creating a product or assessment that is something that they are passionate about. So try to leave it content neutral. Don't make it just about ELA, for example. Give them choice as we do with students. Give them choice. Once you know that they know it, guide them and let them go.

CH: Awesome. Thank you, Kathy, and thanks for the time!

KS: Thank you for having me, and I appreciate you asking me.

CHAPTER 4

TRAILBLAZERS, PIONEERS, LOCALS, AND SETTLERS

Early exploration in America was a risky business. Many of the first to venture West faced treacherous obstacles in their journey to find land and, they hoped, prosperity. Some paid the ultimate price with their lives in pursuit of opportunities in the unknown. While implementing a mobile device initiative isn't nearly as dangerous (one would hope), many of the same principles of those early expansionists hold true when trying to successfully navigate the unknown world of mobile learning.

You need people willing to lead out in front and blaze a trail where no others have gone. You need a group of early innovators willing to follow that trail and pioneer much of this new way of learning without a lot of support. You may have difficult encounters with the locals—the people who have been very comfortable in their ways and see your intrusion on their learning landscape as extremely threatening. Once you've overcome those challenges in your initiative, many of the settlers will come to roost in the new mobile land now that they know it is safe. What follows is a description of these types of staff building off the analogy of expanding into the West.

The Trailblazers

"Here's to the crazy ones." Apple made this Jack Kerouac poem famous with its Think Different commercial in 1997. (Video here: http://mrhook.it/crazy1.) Every campus or district needs a few of these "crazy ones" to be able to blaze the trail for the next group of pioneers. When we first started looking at mobile devices at our elementary schools, we tried all sorts of different scenarios. We put iPads in carts for teachers to share. We had some grade levels decide to split the iPads into classroom sets of five so that kids could rotate or have an opportunity to use the devices in some capacity. And then there was the crazy one.

Laura Wright (@wrightsbatclass on Twitter) had an idea that she proposed to the principal. Rather than have her team use a cart or split up the devices, she would use them all as a class set so that every student had their own. This was a bit of a risky proposition because it meant others on her team would have nothing for a semester while she tested the theory that the devices would be better used in a 1:1 environment versus a shared environment.

The results were amazing. Students were able to keep track of their work, add to existing projects, and not only swim deeper in the SAMR pool (shown in Chapter 2, Figure 2.1 and explained further at http://mrhook.it/pool) but also use higher-order thinking skills by creating and analyzing projects with more depth. When we had Laura come in to talk to our school board, she described a classroom like none other in our district. In all of the other classrooms with technology, students were able to play some learning games and do some internet research, but they were not creating anything because the devices were all shared. The iPad was intended to be an individual device, and that become blatantly evident when we saw the differences in rigor and creativity between Laura's third grade class and the rest.

Laura also kept data on her students' level of engagement and understanding when it came to class work. During the state assessment that year, her students scored about the same when it came to passing the math assessment. However, further inspection revealed that nearly 25% more of her students had actually mastered the content (meaning they didn't only pass, they passed with flying colors). When asked what she had done differently, Laura said, "The only difference about my classroom this year is that all students have a device that allows them to dig deeper into content and math problem solving." In the past those students would have been rewarded with an extra worksheet, but now she was able to give them access to a wide array of tools because of the digital access.

The Pioneers

Just simply blazing a trail isn't really that useful if there is no one following you. The idea of going out in front is finding all the risky areas to avoid and hoping to find some prosperity. In the classroom, it isn't much different. The trailblazers have worked out some of the kinks when it comes to the integration of the mobile devices. Whether it be provisioning apps, connecting to the network, or digital workflow, mobile learning has many moving parts that require patience on first deployment.

The pioneers may not expect as many bumps as the trailblazers, but they must exhibit the same amount of perseverance, if not more, when implementation happens in their classroom. Much of what they "build" in their classroom will be replicated by those that follow them. This group, along with the trailblazers, needs to have ways of quickly providing feedback to those who support them so that any potential roadblocks to learning can be removed.

Finding the pioneers can sometimes be challenging, depending on the campus and the comfort level of technology use with staff. After our trailblazer mentioned earlier showed us the pathway to success with 1:1, we needed to locate some pioneers to come in and create the early settlement. In our LEAP program (http://mrhook.it/leap), we knew that buy-in was a big part of early success. Rather than just blindly handing out devices to students without staff input, we created an application process for those pioneers willing to try 1:1 in their classroom. (See the original application here: http://mrhook.it/wifiapp)

At the high school, we noticed that many of these pioneers were applying from the junior and senior level of courses. Rather than just give those 38 teachers' classes 1:1 iPads, we elected instead to give all juniors and seniors a device (as well as some sophomores taking upper-level classes). This was a very intriguing year in our 1:1, as we had the pioneers and the "settlers" intermingling as well as some pushback from the "locals."

This process was such a success that we replicated it at the elementary level, only we had entire grade-level teams apply from each campus based on who was most ready for it. It turned out that many grade levels differed widely in their approach to digital and mobile learning. On some campuses you had entire teams fighting to be the "chosen one," while on other campuses it almost felt like all the teams except one took one step back as a way to make sure they weren't picked.

From a professional learning prospective, having these pioneers not only onboard but also applying to be a part of this process meant that they would also share their feedback and best practices. They were more inclined to overcome the early obstacles because they were committed to the program. Calling on these pioneers during staff development or even board meetings is an important part of getting the rest of the staff to "migrate" into the territory of mobile learning.

The Locals

Traversing the sometimes treacherous path of mobile learning means that at some point on your journey you have to deal with the locals—the people who are indigenous to the lecture-style, traditional teaching mindset. These encounters and the resistance of those accustomed to traditional methods when asked to consider new ideas can make it difficult during professional learning to get everyone on board.

One particular local I remember quite well. In the spring of 2013, after much surveying of staff, we decided to open up YouTube Safe Search for students. While there can be a lot of mind-numbing videos about squirrels on jet-skis, there is also a large amount of instructional content on there. Want to learn how to do Photoshop? Or maybe just the right way to carve a turkey? It's all on there.

Being a 1:1 iPad school district means that anything we enable on the filter side pretty much goes out to all students, since it's all at their fingertips. It's taken some time for teachers to adjust to this new student-centered focus on learning versus the teacher as "disseminator of all information" model. Again and again, something we noticed during our initiative is that a lecture-based, teacher-at-the-front method of instruction lends itself to more distraction and less educational use of the devices. As teachers shift the knowledge to the students, distraction decreases, and learning with iPads as tools increases. You might be wondering why anyone would be opposed to this concept of teaching style. This may seem like a simple enough switch, but we are asking some of the best and brightest teachers to change everything they have been doing the past 20 or 25 years successfully. Which brings me to January 2013 and the opening of YouTube.

Ten full minutes after announcing that YouTube would be open for students, I received the following email: (Name omitted)

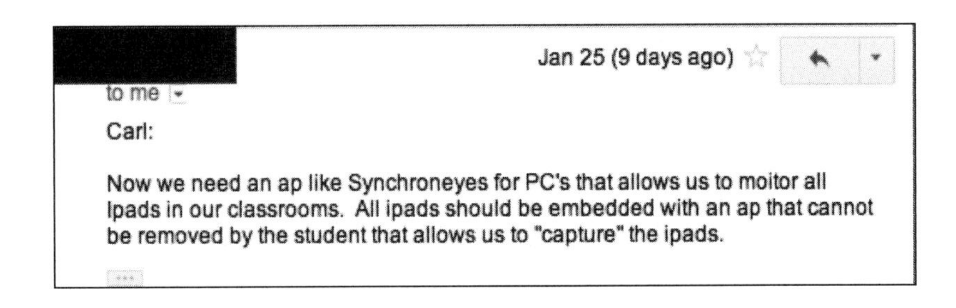
Jan 25 (9 days ago)

to me

Carl:

Now we need an ap like Synchroneyes for PC's that allows us to moitor all Ipads in our classrooms. All ipads should be embedded with an ap that cannot be removed by the student that allows us to "capture" the ipads.

I knew the sender of this email very well, and for the sake of this article we'll just refer to him as Jim. Because Jim was a very accomplished teacher, I realized the worry that he had with all the distraction and possible off-task behavior. I had a list of apps that allow some sort of screen-sheltered management. Apps like Nearpod (http://nearpod.com) or Casper Focus by JAMF (http://www.jamfsoftware.com/products/casper-focus/) allow some form of screen control and embedded lockdown. My gut reaction was to seek out one of these apps as a way to help this him with his teaching. Knowing Jim well, though, I decided on a different approach and response:

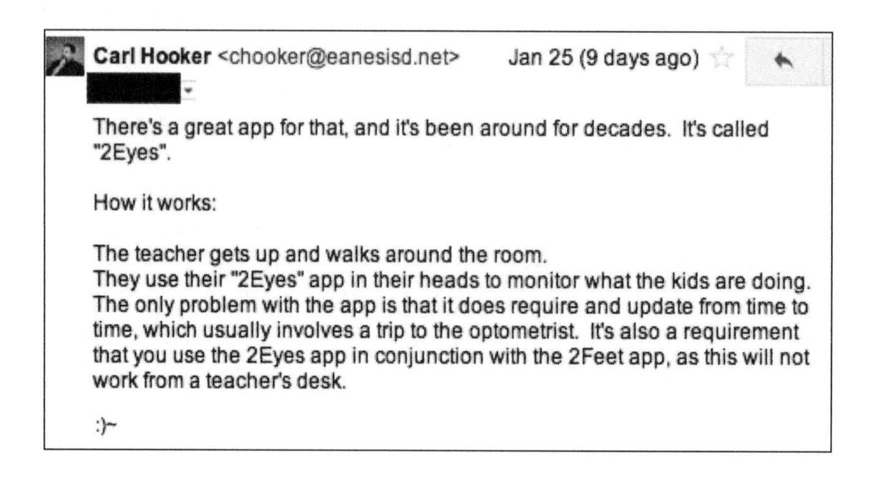
Carl Hooker <chooker@eanesisd.net> Jan 25 (9 days ago)

There's a great app for that, and it's been around for decades. It's called "2Eyes".

How it works:

The teacher gets up and walks around the room.
They use their "2Eyes" app in their heads to monitor what the kids are doing.
The only problem with the app is that it does require and update from time to time, which usually involves a trip to the optometrist. It's also a requirement that you use the 2Eyes app in conjunction with the 2Feet app, as this will not work from a teacher's desk.

:)~

I made sure to include the all important smiley face on my response so that Jim knew I was being somewhat tongue-in-cheek but also sincere when it came to thinking about shifting the pedagogical practice he was employing. I later regretted not adding the statement that you can also use your "iMouth" to enforce restrictions.

In a professional learning workshop, the locals will tend to stand out a bit. While they may only represent 10% to 15% of an organization, they have a powerful reach and voice that can potentially derail an initiative. They will punch holes in others' ideas and claim that "nothing ever works" when it comes to technology. The locals who are not quite as aggressive may passively claim that they "just don't get" technology and show a fixed mindset when it comes to trying out new ideas and concepts.

Indeed, the locals feel that the traditional way of teaching and learning has worked for decades, so why disrupt that in favor of something new and innovative?

The Settlers

Eventually, when the trailblazers and pioneers have overcome any pain points and struggles, the settlers will follow behind. This group represents the majority of staff on your campus, and they are somewhat skeptical of what lies ahead. For them, traveling down this road needs to have a purpose. Using technology to enhance learning sounds great, but does it solve a problem for them, too? Otherwise, why leave the lands in which they are comfortable?

There will still be some struggles as they adjust to this new land. New tools to learn and new challenges to face, but those that follow will see the value of moving if given the right amount of professional learning opportunities and support from leadership. In your average professional learning session, the settlers will represent anywhere from 60% to 80% of the people in the room. They may decide to take an active part in the learning, or they may take more of a "wait and see" approach to whatever it is you are trying to show them.

It's important not only to acknowledge the settlers within your organization, but also to showcase those settlers who do well in this new environment. Many school teacher leaders live in this category, and they carry with them a weight of respect from the other teachers on the campus. Having the settlers in the camp of mobile learning means that you now have the majority of staff living and breathing in the mobile learning landscape.

No matter which group you encounter along your mobile journey, quality professional learning that is dynamic and plays to each group's strengths will help make your road less bumpy. There will still be times when you'll have to pause, perhaps during a device refresh—but never stop striving to expand and move forward. The balance of the trailblazers and the locals also plays an important role. Since the trailblazers will take risks and run with them, they need to be given the freedom to do so. On the other hand, the locals can't be

BRAIN BREAK

Reverse Charades

Materials Needed: None

Concept: Playing charades with a twist to get the brain thinking

Audience Size: 10+

Set-up: Have participants partner up. One person starts acting out an activity and the other person asks, "Hey, (name)! What are you doing?" The person then responds with something different than what they are doing. The other person then must act out what was said, and they change roles and continue the game.

Example: (Person acting like they are flying a kite) "Hey Bill! What are you doing?" Bill responds, "I'm riding a bike." Then the partner begins acting like they are riding a bike and Bill asks the question, "Hey Ted! What are you doing?" and so on.

the ones holding back progress and change. Leadership needs to set expectations around a mobile device initiative and then support those expectations with professional learning to move all the groups forward. Once that expectation is set, the opportunities for providing high-quality and differentiated professional learning to aid in the professional growth of staff will be almost limitless.

CHAPTER 5

TIME FOR CHANGE AND THE SAMR MODEL

As we identified in Chapter 4, you know there are all sorts of different adult learners within and throughout your organization. From the trailblazers to the settlers to the "restless locals," the focus of professional learning is how to get them on board with mobile learning. But that's just the first step. When the settlers finally traveled to their new land, how did they sustain life and success? A lot of that comes with learning the new land, growing cycles, seasonal changes, indigenous species and pests, and so on.

In a classroom that has settled into the mobile learning realm, it's not much different. There will be times when the internet isn't so great—bugs and glitches, distraction, and students testing the boundaries of what's appropriate to do in class and what isn't. Keeping those settlers attuned to these activities is important, but you also want them to grow and improve. It's one thing to get comfortable and survive in a new environment. It's a whole new thing altogether to thrive in it. In this section, we'll look at a human being's capacity for growth and change as well as how the SAMR model could help promote some of this improvement.

What Is a Person's Capacity for Growth?

Every year for the past 4 years I've done multiple different diets and challenges to help me lose weight. After 40 years of bad habits, I attempt to undo all of that with a totally revamped diet or exercise plan that is completely opposite of the way of I've been living my life. For several years I've even tried to get social media into the act (post here: http://mrhook.it/diet) by having friends and family participate in the form of a virtual support group. Although I experienced short-term success in these weight loss challenges, it was never very sustainable. I would pick up little changes in my routine, but because the challenges were 12 to 16 weeks in length, I knew there was an ending point and didn't internalize any of the changes or habits.

That was until this past year. I decided to embark on a different type of challenge, one that wasn't quite so short-term. So, for the entirety of 2015 (and now round 2 in 2016) I have been part of a group that supports slow, steady weight loss. Rather than try and lose 10% of your body weight in 12 weeks, we set a goal of 12% over a year. Add to that the fact that you had to lose a minimum of 1% a month to have a "good month" or risk a penalty, and you can see how this challenge became much more internalized that others in the past. Just as in teaching, we're always going to have bad days when it comes to diet. However, with a long-term goal in front of us, many more people experienced success. Not only that, but they maintained their success after the challenge had finished. In some ways, this slow and steady goal created a lifestyle change.

So what does a diet have to do with teaching and professional learning? Much like my diets, people can experience short-term success with mobile learning. Perhaps they have a great project that goes well or have the kids on some sort of formative assessment platform that gives them instant feedback. Regardless of what it is, they experience a short burst of success, but then immediately revert back to traditional teaching methods when the project or activity is over. They didn't internalize it—they saw it as a temporary thing to do (like a 12-week diet), and after that they could go back to their comfort zone.

People Need Time to Change

During our first year of 1:1, we reached the midterm break and I visited a few classrooms that had been a part of our pilot. Some were doing great things with devices; others had reverted to their old ways and traditional teaching. I was astounded and frustrated at the slow pace of change and asked to have a meeting with the campus principal at the time to discuss this with her.

"People need time to change," she said. "Not everyone has the capacity to change their teaching habits overnight. Most of these teachers have been very successful with the traditional methods of teaching, so asking them to change and adjust takes time and buy-in."

Her words were a dose of cold water, but they were also what I needed to hear and understand at that time. Not everyone succeeds with change. In fact, when I started doing some research on this, I came across this article in Forbes about how many people succeed at their New Year's resolutions (http://mrhook.it/nyr). It turns out, according to the University of Scranton, that only around 8% of people actually succeed in changing a part of themselves that they set forth in a resolution. Think about that. Those are *self-imposed* goals, not goals or actions foisted onto them. Even with that initial motivation, only 8% succeeded. Yet I'm expecting a staff of 200 to change based on my imposed goals. How could I be so unaware of the importance of capacity for change?

Rather than continue in frustration, I decided to investigate what made people successfully achieve change and what tools I could give them to both motivate them and make them more successful in integrating mobile devices in their classroom.

Baby Steps

When trying to get my toddler to learn a new skill, such as walking, I couldn't expect her to just stand up and walk to me. There were several attempts at standing, then falling, then standing again. Often, she would need a table or chair leg to hold onto to steady herself before proceeding forward. She knew she had succeeded when she was able to ultimately waddle toward me, successfully traversing the great expanse between the coffee table and the chair I was sitting on at the time.

What makes the analogy of "baby steps" for change so great is that it's very visual. I didn't put my child in the middle of the room and yell at her to stand up and walk until she did it. I gave her goals and scaffolds of support to let her have small successes and failures along the way until she achieved her goal. Professional learning and capacity for change should be treated in much the same way when a teacher is being expected to integrate mobile devices for the first time. Some teachers (just like some toddlers) will take to it much more quickly than others, but your goal should always be that everyone will be "walking" on their own eventually.

When looking at our own staff, we tried to have them self-identify how comfortable they were with mobile devices in their classroom and how much change they could tolerate. There were always a few teachers who seemed to say "I'm too old to learn this" or "I will retire before this comes to pass." Regardless of the reasons, some staff just aren't ready to take those first few baby steps, while others feel like they can just stand up and run with it.

During a mobile device initiative, it's a good idea to identify some "baby steps" that will help teachers feel successful along this journey. These may be just simple substitutive tasks (more on that in a minute), but that does get them comfortable standing up on their own. Another part of that journey means overcoming the fear of taking the risk of having technology in their class-room. While it can be a powerful tool for learning, there is also potential for negative outcomes.

Technology, the Great Amplifier

The power of technology in the hands of students can be both a terrifying and incredible thing to behold. Students previously left to doze in the back of the room or who were too shy to take part in a discussion can now be heard. Subjects that pique students' interest are no longer road kill on the way to the land of high-stakes tests. Even the most boring of interactions have an uptick of engagement when technology is involved.

I recently witnessed one of our 1:1 fourth grade classes engaging with those dreaded "fractions worksheets." I walked in and the class was silent, almost in rapture if you will, with their worksheets. I even heard one of the students exclaim, "This is fun!" This was not some sort of strange *Twilight Zone* episode—it was the teacher making use of his newly delivered iPads to turn an everyday mundane task into one filled with excitement. Now, although this is clearly a substitutive task on Dr. Ruben Puentedura's SAMR model (http://mrhook.it/samr1), the participation was incredible to behold. Every student wanted to share what they had learned, because they were excited about learning.

Although the nuance of the device does play a role in this engagement, I wanted to see if it had even deeper impact, so I headed across our district to take part in an interview with a third grade 1:1 teacher, Laura Wright, and the local news. I've mentioned Laura before and even highlighted her iBook *The Life of an Eanes Pioneer Child* (http://mrhook.it/pioneer). Her statement to me that having iPads had "completely transformed the way I teach and my motivation to teach and learn" left me both excited and flummoxed. Surely, all the amazement and wonder at the introduction of a magical device must have some downside? Well, it turns out, it does. Two weeks before my experi-ences at the local elementary campuses, I was starting to hear story after story from some concerned parents of our secondary students about distraction and gaming in the classroom. Although I knew that the age differences could have led to more negative outcomes for the older students, this wasn't the case in *all* middle school classrooms, just in some. I decided to dig a little deeper into why some teachers "just got it," while other struggled with it.

During the course of my investigation, I came across an "On Point" radio show by NPR with some educational leaders discussing various experiences with 1:1 tablets in their schools. During the course of the interview, someone called in saying that he was "entirely appalled" at the direction schools were going in with technology. During the course of his rant, he made the claim that these devices "cover up bad teaching." Over the course of the last several years of seeing 1:1 in action, I'm afraid I have to disagree. In fact, as discovered from the previously mentioned situations, 1:1 technology seems to amplify teaching ability.

Let's take the first two examples. Although both of these teachers were at different levels of having iPads in their classroom, their students still used them appropriately. In the case of Ms. Wright's class, the technology had almost become invisible—just a tool students used to expand on their own learning. In the latter example, it turns out that a few teachers hadn't really accounted for the idea that this access carries with it some level of expectation of use. It had actually amplified what had been a flawed system in classroom management. Unlike what the NPR caller said, bad teaching is easier to cover up when the students are forced to turn off all technology, sit in rows, and quietly listen to the lecture.

What can we learn from this? Those of us entering the world of 1:1 learning must prepare for the messiness that comes with such implementation. Continual professional learning for your staff braving this frontier is a given if you want it to succeed. You must expect that with the great advantages to learning that have been gained, there also come some ugly truths that must be faced at times. Although it has its flaws and shouldn't be considered the be-all and end-all of learning models, the SAMR model does help teachers visual technology use with their students. (For more, see the SAMR swimming pool in Chapter 2.)

Professional Learning via the SAMR Model

Having a good model to build off of is just one step in getting transformation to happen with mobile learning. Just talking about the model and how things "should be" in the classroom isn't enough. I think that in order to truly embrace this new student-centered style of mobile learning, professional development should reflect this model in terms of practice as well. So ,with that in mind, I've attempted to break down professional learning in terms of the SAMR model, realizing that just as in the classroom, redefinition can't happen at every training event.

Substitution With Professional Learning

We've all attended these kind of sessions. In some cases I would say the "sit 'n' get" session is the staple of most conferences or in-district professional learning. Technology is used as a substitute (if at all), and the teachers are "talked at" during the entire presentation. Just as in the classroom, there are times to have these types of sessions. One example that comes to mind is our new teacher orientation. We can have anywhere between 50 and 100 teachers in a room and try to feed our district culture and mindset to them. These have been effective over the years even at the substitutive level, but many teachers leave feeling as if they have been drinking from a fire hose and can barely remember what they have learned.

It seems that most types of professional learning that involves learning facts or tools does center around substitutive tasks. Taking notes (either with or without technology) is about the only thing that you can ask attendees to do. In a quick staff meeting or lunch gathering, that might be all you can do with the time allowed (though I'll argue later that time shouldn't be a constraint when it comes to engaging professional learning). So how do you take the standard "sit 'n' get" PD session and make it a little more transformative? Just as in the classroom, the answer means giving up some amount of control to the "students," in this case the teaching staff.

Augmentation With Professional Learning

As Dr. Puentedura mentions, augmentation is when technology enhances a substitutive task. The environment is still very teacher-centric, but now technology is allowing the teacher a few advantages that couldn't have happened with the non-tech substitute. Take my example of the new teacher orientation. In previous years, when I presented the district's R.U.G. (Responsible Use Guidelines), I did so in a PowerPoint presentation format. I would talk at the teachers for 10 or 15 minutes about what they should or shouldn't do when it comes to technology, and then save a minute or two at the end for questions.

This past year I tried a different method of disseminating this information. I made it into a game show using the Kahoot! app (www.getkahoot.com) and had all the new staff take our their phones or use whatever device they had on them to answer a series of questions centered around the R.U.G. This helped me accomplish the task of getting them to learn the material while also making it much more engaging for those in the room. Many of the new teachers felt much more comfortable asking questions, and I was able to gauge the room for level of understanding based on responses to the prompt. Rather than spend 2 or 3 minutes talking about email protocol, if I can tell the group already understands what that is based on their responses, I can then move on to other discussion items like social media use, which generally brings about a mixed set of responses.

I could have done this by having the teachers raise their hands or shout out answers, but I truly wouldn't be able to "see" what everyone was thinking with a technology-based formative assessment tool. Technology augmented the training, and I was able to adjust it on the fly based on the knowledge of the group.

Modification With Professional Learning

Modification means that the use of technology in your professional learning environment now begins to lead to a significant redesign of how it is delivered and learned. A typical workshop setting with chairs and tables in rows generally doesn't work for this style of learning. With this shift from the previous two methods of PD, the "weight" of responsibility of learning falls more on the staff attending than the person presenting.

Typically you'll see rooms set up with round tables where staff can work on a task or challenge. Introducing technology concepts in this format is far more successful in terms of actual classroom integration, because the teacher is actually able to experience things from the standpoint of a student in their classroom.

Format is just one step, though, as this is "modification" using technology to redesign a task. One of my favorite tools to use for this is Padlet (www.padlet.com). This is a free online bulletin board that may seem somewhat substitutive at face value, but in actuality, it comes down to how it is being used. Let's take my example of the new teacher orientation and my previous stand-and-deliver format accentuated by the use of some technology.

Rather than me quizzing them on the various aspects of the R.U.G., I could now break them into teams and have them not only analyze the R.U.G. but also post different ways the guidelines could be broken on a centralized Padlet wall. Again, if I leave it at that level, it could be seen as a substitutive task. I mean, couldn't they just put sticky notes on a wall? What makes using a tool like Padlet so much more powerful is the fact that users can post videos on the wall. So now, instead of them just writing down some ideas, they actually create a video demonstrating the specific guideline and how it might be broken. The technology allowed for a significant amount of redesign and actual learning outcome. Many of those teachers will never forget the guidelines because they were forced to teach the class to understand them—*and,* because it's on a live online link, it can stay with them as an archive to refer back to throughout the year in case they have some sort of question or concern.

Redefinition With Professional Learning

Reaching the status of redefinition as defined by Dr. Puentedura means that now technology has allowed for tasks never previously conceived. In terms of professional learning, that becomes a challenge because a majority of professional learning workshops are scripted. That means there is an agenda with an intended set of outcomes that the presenter or facilitator guides the students through.

Taking something to the level of redefinition would be somewhat uncomfortable to the standard adult learning that relies on the "sit 'n' get" philosophy most organizations employ with their professional learning strategies. In a truly redefined session, the learner would be in charge not only of their own learning, but of successfully reaching outcomes using tools that the presenter may not be familiar with.

As a presenter, I've only had this happen a handful of times, but when it happens, you can almost see the lightbulbs coming on with teachers. One of the most successful examples of this didn't happen in a standard workshop, but actually in a classroom with students.

Over the course of my career, I've sometimes been asked to go to other schools and districts not only to consult, but also to work with teachers on strategies of integration around technology. One such visit had me right in the middle of a first grade classroom that had recently received their 1:1 iPads. The teacher admitted to me that while she was very strong instructionally with her students, she didn't know a lot about technology. However, she was open to trying new things if it meant making the kids learn a concept better. In other words, she didn't just want to do technology for technology's sake.

During this particular visit, she and I had worked on some tools for the kids to learn ahead of time as they prepared for my visit to the classroom. She took many of the tools and apps from our prior time together and really moved quickly in integrating in her classroom. While there was not a lot of transformational learning taking place, the students seemed comfortable with the technology and were willing to try new things. When she invited me into her classroom, she explained to me that she was trying to do two things:

1. Have the students learn more about bats.
2. Use an app called Chalkboard to help them demonstrate their understanding.

I was not familiar with the app at all, so going in as a trainer, I felt at a disadvantage. However, I knew that it can't be just about the app, so I tried to go in with an open mind. She quickly explained to the kids that they were to "explore" the app for a period of time, and then she would give them a task.

During the exploratory phase of this lesson, I'd say the students were pretty much all over the map. Some were trying new things, some were lost, and some were using apps they weren't supposed to. She looked at me with a look of desperation, and the first grade teacher inside me kicked in. Seeing that leaving the kids in exploratory mode without direction was causing problems, I asked the students to draw their best bat in the app. This was a very substitutive use of the technology, but it did accomplish some of her two objectives.

As students continued to build and iterate on their bats, something started to happen. First, all of the students became much more focused on the task at hand. Second, many of them began to experiment with various features of the app. One student realized you could import a picture from your camera roll as the background. This lit a fire of excitement with the students as they soon realized they could put themselves (via a selfie) in the picture with their bat. Many of the students began acting out a scared look with an invisible bat over their shoulder and adapting it even further.

Then, one very innocent (but precocious) student told me he wished there was a way that he could put the bat in its more natural habitat of a cave. I stopped the class to ask for their feedback as to how he could best accomplish what he was doing. Some students suggested drawing the cave, and others suggested drawing it out on paper first and then taking a picture of it. One student, who could barely contain himself, waved his hand wildly about. When I called on him he stood up and said, "There's this thing called 'the internets' where satellites connect and let you search for things."

BRAIN BREAK

1, 2, 3

Materials Needed: None

Concept: Demonstrating differences between verbal learners and kinesthetic learners in a fun way that also celebrates failure.

Audience Size: Any size (but the bigger the more entertaining). Must be in partners.

Set-up: In partners, have partner A say "1", then partner B says "2", then partner A says "3", then partner B starts over with "1" and so on. Do this for about 30 seconds but also encourage groups to "celebrate failure" by putting their hands high in the air and shouting out "WOO HOO!". Once you've finished one round introduce a variable. Instead of saying "1" they must clap and still say 2 and 3. Then in the next round, keep the clap and substitute "2" with a stomp. Then in the final round have them snap for the "3" making it completely physical all the while shouting out "WOO HOO!" whenever they fail.

The students became abuzz with excitement and quickly set to spelling out c-a-v-e on their web search site to find photos of caves. Several students found photos but struggled figuring out how to get the photos from the internet to their background in the Chalkboard app. Rather than telling them, I had students discuss how best to do this. A few students suggested they could help, so with a quick switch of the Apple TV in the front of the class, I put the student's iPad on the projection screen so he could show us his method for accomplishing this. The students immediately tried to replicate his actions of "holding down" to activate the save menu and then opening it in the other app.

While many failed at first, other students jumped in to help them work through it. In the period of 30 minutes, the class had gone from an exploratory lesson, to one with some direction, to one where the students were the lead learners (and teachers). The teacher looked to me with a look of amazement and asked, "How did you know that was what they would do? That was almost magical!" I revealed to her the truth. I didn't know anything about the app they were working on or their final outcomes before I set foot in the classroom. I did, however, use my experience as a teacher (just like her) to guide the lesson in a certain direction while allowing the students to redefine their own learning outcomes.

This particular example doesn't happen every day in the classroom or in a workshop, but the main strategies used can be applied to both areas. Setting some expectations and then getting out of the way of the student can create outcomes and tasks not previously conceived. In the case of the classroom just discussed, that clearly happened, and the amount of ownership the students felt in their own learning was palpable.

Setting Goals With Professional Learning

So you've done your best to build time into the schedule, and created an environment that invites transformational learning. Setting goals both within the organization at increments of 1, 3, and 5 years will help guide the areas of growth and the implementation of growth. As I've pointed out already, only certain percentages of staff will take to the change in the first year.

Part of continuing the growth of staff knowledge is to figure out how to scale past that initial percentage of trailblazers into the majority of teachers integrating at a higher level. Building in realistic timeframes while not loading the teachers up with many other initiatives is a key to this success. While our initiative and encouraging student-centered learning and differentiation with integration of technology was an important part of our district goals, it was also one of many other goals that were imposed on teachers at the same time, which clouded the vision and the timeline somewhat.

In Figure 5.1, I've shown what an "ideal" timeline of integration would look like with continual job-embedded support, some level of expectation from leadership, and not a lot of other initiatives going on at the same time. That means that your laggard teachers (representing 10% to 16% of staff) won't really embrace the integration until year 4.

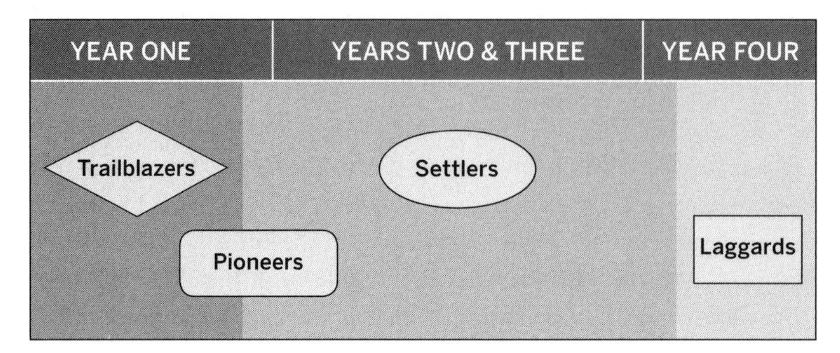

Figure 5.1 Integration timeline

I tell you this not to give you a concrete timeline to build off of, as every district is different, but instead to help you build a framework of goals and expectations of your professional learning around mobile device integration. As we've seen from our percentages, some people may take many years before becoming open to the idea of using mobile devices in their classroom. Others may take even longer, because of either fear or lack of belief that the technology has any impact in their classroom. Once you finally have those people on board, you have successfully navigated your way through change management on a large scale.

CHAPTER 6

FINDING LEARNING OPPORTUNITIES

As a classroom teacher, I always felt like time was continually being compressed. I would always start the year with the best of intentions in terms of teaching content, but then at some point in the middle of year things would become unraveled. Maybe it was a particularly challenging student added to my class, some extra job duties thrown at me, or a new initiative by the district that ended up eating up a majority of my time with my students.

Knowing that time is finite with students, most districts (including ours for the most part) try to cram all of their professional learning into either the beginning of summer or the end. This practice has been tried and true for those districts on the traditional calendar. Schools that have adopted year-round calendars see the benefit of year-round schooling in not only the students' capacity to learn but also the increase in opportunities for adult learning. But what do you do if you are on a traditional school calendar? How do you find opportunities for learning throughout the year? Let's look at these questions and others that may arise when planning professional learning, as well as some ideas and solutions.

Where Does Learning Happen?

One of my favorite questions to ask a group of adults is to identify places where learning happens or where they go to create. Many will identify a soft chair at home, sitting on their porch, or visiting the local coffee shop. Our classrooms and professional learning spaces are not necessarily environments that are conducive to learning. The traditional "desks in rows" design was great for disseminating information to individuals and an efficient way for custodial staff to clean in between the desks.

The "all-in-one" desk itself is really isolating and uncomfortable in its design. I'll get more into learning spaces and the classroom in book 4, but we need to consider learning spaces when we train adults. too. I've visited a few districts that have designed professional learning rooms with comfortable chairs on wheels and movable tables. However, many districts don't have that luxury and use whatever space available to them (usually a library, cafeteria. or classroom) to host teacher inservice.

I think we as educators can be trapped by our own past experiences when it comes to where learning takes place. Since our last years of learning as adults happened in a college classroom, usually lasting for a 3-hour chunk, we do the same thing as professionals—having professional development from 8:30 to 11:30, with a break for lunch, followed by another 3-hour chunk starting around 12:30. The only indicator that teachers are getting professional learning is a sign-in sheet, generally in the morning and afternoon, that indicates their presence in the room. It's almost as if just being the room means they are getting the training they need. Having attended and presented hundreds of professional learning sessions, I can tell you that for some people, while they may be physically present in the room, they aren't really active learners.

How Do You Know They Are Learning If They Aren't in the Room?

Knowing that learning can happen anywhere and anytime, I proposed an idea that I had learned about from some other innovative school districts—that teachers could get credit online in a couple of different formats. One was taking an online iTunes U course where they created actual classroom projects to turn in as proof of learning. The other was the idea that teachers could attend online Twitter chats for professional development credit. After proposing both of these ideas, I was approached by a fellow administrator (who oversaw much of the professional learning in the district), who asked me, "How do you know they are learning if they aren't in the room?" My response quite simply was, "How do you know they are learning if they are in the room?"

Simply being somewhat attentive during a 6-hour workshop means that you have learned something just by being there. I've seen teachers in the back of rooms cutting our letters for a bulletin board, grading papers, checking Facebook, and even shopping online. I'm not sure that in those cases being present guarantees any learning is taking place. Adults can still get learning done while doing all of these things, but I'd hazard a guess that your professional development isn't that compelling if someone in your audience just spent 30 minutes updating their latest Pinterest board with birthday party ideas for a 4-year old.

Online Courses for PD

I've tried the online course model a couple of different ways. The first was very much intended to be a "flipped" concept for professional development. Teachers would watch a series of videos on various topics and tools, and then we would convene in a physical space as group to spend time applying what we had learned. Although well intended, this ended up being a failure, as many teachers didn't watch the videos before attending the workshop as I had hoped. As a result, we spent most of the workshop going over what the training videos went over, frustrating those who had done their preparation. Although I gave teachers credit for attending and taking part in the "flipped PD" experiment, I'd say this method for professional learning wasn't very effective for those who attended.

For my second iteration, I decided to stick with a solely online concept. I've had some experiences with these courses using iTunes U, with the parents in the community taking my "Digital Parenting 101" course (http://mrhook.it/101—must be on an iOS device to view). However, there were negatives attached to that course: All you had to do was pass a quiz at the end of each section and participate in the community forums to qualify for credit.

To truly make the learning embedded, the course enrollees must demonstrate their learning of the topic or tool in a variety of formats. These series of challenges would be open-ended in terms of content but intended to showcase a particular tool or app while enabling and encouraging the enrollees to integrate their own curriculum into the completed projects. I found a far greater success rate in terms of completion using this model, and the feedback from those who completed the course indicated that they felt that they learned quite a bit more because they were forced to demonstrate understanding, rather than sitting and listening to someone tell them about a particular tool. While there is still some room for improvement on this model (there was virtually no collaboration between the students), it was a good next step into the realm of online professional learning.

Twitter Chats for PD Credit

One of the more innovative ideas I've heard districts try is the idea that staff participate in six twitter chats to earn their 6 hours of credit. I first learned about this from our neighboring district in Manor, Texas, who regularly hosted a weekly twitter chat using the #ManorISD hashtag. In the spring of 2014, a small group of teachers offered to participate in a six-part series of twitter chats using the #EanesChat hashtag. We had multiple people moderate the chat based on their area of expertise and had a wide range of teachers from kindergarten to AP Calculus participating in the chat.

This was a great first model, but it lacked some of the flexibility that comes with online learning. In some ways, it wasn't really embracing learning "anytime," even though learning could happen anywhere. For the next iteration, we adapted a model that had been shared with us by Lewisville ISD, so that teachers could attend any chats that they wanted to and could focus on some that were more around their subject area. Then, after they completed the chats, they would fill out the form to show not only that they participated, but that they also had identified takeaways from the chats that they would use in their classroom. Not only were they accountable for their learning, but they also had ideas they could put into practice right away in their classroom.

Job-Embedded Learning for Just-in-Time Training

Before the launch of our initial iPad pilot at Westlake High School, the state of Texas had decided to cut the educational funding budget, resulting in the loss of 100,000 teaching jobs. For many districts, including ours, that meant cutting support staff such as instructional coaches or educational technologists. So, on the brink of rolling out a few thousand devices to students, I was asked to cut my department from a team of nine to a team of four.

BRAIN BREAK

Yes, And

Materials Needed: None

Concept: Using the improve concept of "Yes, And" to contribute positively to a conversation.

Audience Size: Any size

Set-up: In partners, discuss an idea or topic on which you may have differing viewpoints. In the first round, start every sentence with "Yeah, but." Do this for about a minute, then ask the participants to stop and have the same conversation, only this time starting each sentence with "Yes, and." Discuss the differences in their conversations and the outcomes of their discussions.

Example Scenarios: You and your partner are planning the end-of-year staff party. Or a more difficult scenario would be: One partner plays the role of someone against the use of mobile devices, and the other sees the value.

As a result, most the effort that went into training had to happen at the high school, and other campuses were left without much in terms of technology integration. With the expansion of our 1:1 into all the campuses, principals saw the power and potential of having this job-embedded position available on each campus. Educational Technologists (affectionately referred to as an "iVenger" based on the Marvel comics series of action heroes) are very much the face of technology on the campus. They help coordinate repairs, train teachers, work with parents, teach students, and help with campus web and social media presence.

Most districts can't afford to have a professional position such as an ed tech on each campus, but having someone as the face of the initiative is invaluable. In my previous book focused on campus leadership, I wrote that it is imperative that the principal own the initiative. However, with the many other duties that principals have to fulfill on a daily basis, there also needs to be a person on campus who acts as a "point" person. We were fortunate to have a very tech-savvy librarian (Carolyn Foote) at our high school to help us with our pilot year. She was able to gather data about issues students and teachers were facing as well as share stories of success.

Every campus traditionally has a librarian on staff. With the transition to more digital text, in some ways, the library is shrinking in how it was previously used. Even the title of "librarian" has now transformed into a more modernized "library media specialist" on many campuses. At any rate, this point person should be available for just-in-time training throughout the school day. They should also advertise pockets of time throughout the year where training over a particular application or strategy can be featured in a short, bite-sized segment.

Even though they come in small doses, some of our best-attended training sessions are "Lunch 'n' Learns" and "Appy Hours." I'll address the "Appy Hour" concept in more detail in the next chapter, but the basic concept of a Lunch 'n' learn is to give staff an opportunity to pick up a tidbit about an app or have a discussion around a new program. They grab their lunch, and in 30 minutes or less, we go over a single tool or concept. In some cases we've even used these to host facilitated discussions on topics from classroom management in a classroom full of mobile devices to ideas on how to get started "flipping" some content in a video format online. We've also used lunch 'n' learns as opportunities to introduce a new feature in a program like Google Drive or perhaps a new formative assessment app like Kahoot! (http://getkahoot.com).

Training With TPACK in Mind

Every district has a set of initiatives it's trying to push forward with staff and students. Not all of these initiatives have direct impact when it comes to technology integration and mobile learning. However, I'd argue that every training session, regardless of topic, is an opportunity to model effective technology integration. There seems to be a natural dichotomous split—"technology-based" training versus "curricular-based" training—but they don't need to be mutually exclusive.

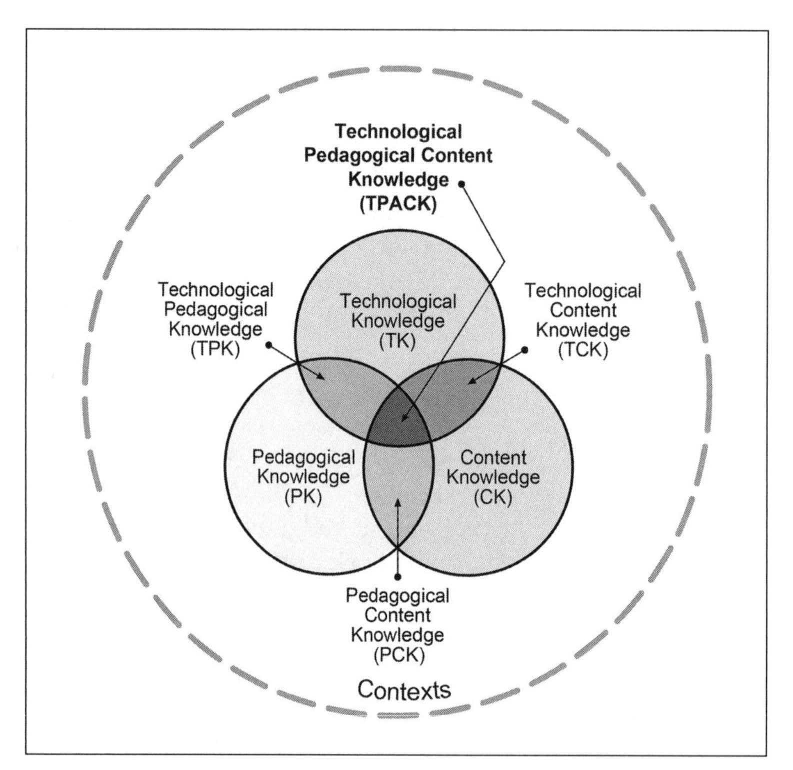

Figure 6.1 TPACK model

The TPACK model (www.tpack.org) really addresses the idea that a goal of teaching and learning should be a blend of technological knowledge, pedagogical knowledge and content knowledge (Figure 6.1). As with the Redefinition level of the SAMR model, not every lesson can be a perfect blend of all of these, but that should be a goal when creating learning for adults or students.

Think about this: A training that just covers technology tools with no curricular or instructional application is a very shallow way of covering the effect of mobile learning in the classroom. I've been to many a session that touts "60 apps in 60 minutes" as kind of a shotgun approach to covering as many apps as possible in the hope that a teacher in the audience finds one to grab hold of. I'm not dismissing these types of sessions as shallow, as I do think they have a place in staff professional learning. Staff need to be exposed to a variety of apps, considering the variety of ages and subjects they cover, but this can't be the sole source of training when it comes to mobile learning.

The counter to that is a curricular-focused training with no technology or real instructional ideas embedded. I've seen this before when you purchase a textbook from a big-time publisher and they bring in a former classroom teacher to show you how to use the textbook. Just as with the technology-only sessions, this is a missed opportunity with staff by focusing on just one part of the Technological, Pedagogical, and Content Knowledge (TPACK) framework. We are all experiencing a sort of "time famine" when it comes to the day-to-day learning that happens in schools. So why not integrate multiple types of knowledge into a training session when you have the teachers in front of you?

Here are just a couple of quick examples of ways to do this. Obviously every district has it's own set of goals and missions, but I'd bet there is some component of that mission that involves integrating technology (otherwise you wouldn't be reading this book).

Example 1: Ignite a Staff Meeting

Next time you have a staff meeting planned, take the first 15 minutes to have three different staff members share something they are doing in their classrooms that is engaging students. This does not have to be technology focused, but the very fact that teachers are sharing images, slides, and resources from their lessons will model some level of integration. Doing these sessions in an Ignite! format (5 minutes max to present their findings) means that staff don't need to feel pressured to run an entire training. The added bonus to this is that various staff members also begin to be seen as experts around a particular tool or idea, which builds leadership capacity among staff.

Example 2: Take a PLC Online

The professional learning community, or PLC, concept has really grown in schools over the years. At it's core, the PLC helps leverage best practices from other teaching the same subject or grade level as well as guaranteeing a viable curriculum. Many districts (mine included) use this time at first to cover common assessments and data of how students are doing on certain learning objectives. Although this is a perfect use of PLC time together, it shouldn't be limited to just looking at assessment data. This is also a time to discuss instructional strategies and technology integration (think the other parts of TPACK). One of the better uses I've seen of this recently is an entire campus leveraging Google Communities (http://plus.google.com/communities) to put their PLC online. The principal is invited to be a part of each of these communities and see the resources and interactions shared asynchronously among members of the PLC.

Example 3: Make Formative Assessments Digital

Many curriculum resources have some assessment component. This could be in the form of a chapter or unit test, or maybe just a typical scantron-based final exam to check content knowledge. Formative assessments, when used correctly, can be a powerful tool for gauging students' knowledge of certain contents and learning objectives. Digitizing these makes the results more dynamic and instant. Teachers no longer needs to lug an entire briefcase full of papers home to grade every night when they can use an online tool like Socrative (http://socrative.com) or Kahoot! (http://getkahoot.com) to quickly gather data and make an adjustment to what is happening in the classroom.

Badges

One recent trend in professional learning is using a system of badges to identify which teachers have completed various levels of training. The idea is simple: A staff member completes a challenge or set of challenges on their own and turns them in to earn a badge. For example, a teacher could earn a "Google Calendar" badge by showing how to send invites, add attachments, change views and colors, and so on within a Google Calendar.

The advantages to this system are that it gives teachers a somewhat tangible item to show progress, and it really feeds on their competitiveness. The badges can be worth hours of PD credit and in some cases include a chance to win a prize or two. To make this type of professional learning system even more effective, the campus administrator needs to make a minimum level of badges mandatory for all staff. Otherwise, you'll have just the same 10% to 15% of vanguard staff members completing the challenges.

Although I've seen badging systems primarily focused on technology tools (the "Technological Knowledge" component in TPACK), there is no reason it has to be just focused on technology integration. Badge systems can work for PLCs ("Collaborative team" badge) to Social-emotional learning ("SEL" badge for conflict resolution) to flexible learning environments ("Coffee shop" badge for the classroom that looks most like a coffee shop). I do think that starting with the basic technology tools and covering district systems (like online grade book or web design) is a great way to knock out some low-hanging fruit and really get at more in-depth learning when you do have face-to-face training planning. Knowing that everyone in the room has earned the "Google Docs" badge means that you can now collaborate online and have some common vocabulary when discussing technological knowledge.

Student-Led PD

One of the most effective models of professional learning that I've ever witnessed is when students train teachers on a concept or technology tool. As an adult in a training session, I'm somewhat skeptical of what other adults can offer me in terms of how I can improve my teaching. I equate this to a parent telling another parent better ways to raise their child, it's intensely personal in many ways.

Students on the other hand have an innocence to them that tends to make adults a little more open to the concept they are teaching (assuming that all teachers like kids, which I realize could be a big assumption.) To test this theory, I employed my then nearly 3-year old daughter Sophia (Figure 6.2) to lead some training on the basics of an iPad. Her audience? High school teachers.

Sophia showed them the ins and outs of a few built-in apps on the device, with an extremely limited vocabulary. I know this was a bit of a schtick, using my own daughter to show them features, but the effect was palpable. The ease with which she could navigate the device showed them that while they may be skeptical of some of its uses, they couldn't deny that there was soon going to be a whole army of Sophias gracing the doorway of their classrooms.

Taking this student-led professional learning concept a bit further (and deeper), it doesn't take long to imagine other scenarios where students could help lead professional learning on a campus for teachers and students. One middle school campus took this a step further and actually reserved two days out of the school year for students and teachers to flip roles. Early in the year, students (mostly eighth graders) would train both new teachers and students on some of the basic apps that are used regularly in class. At the end of the year, a day was reserved to showcase some innovative uses of technology and learning. While these are great first attempts on this student-led concept, I think there is some real potential in outsourcing parts of professional learning to our own students in the future.

Figure 6.2 Sophia leads some iPad training

CHAPTER 7

COLLABORATE, SHARE, AND SHOWCASE

Sharing and collaborating with peers can be one of the most powerful ways to learn, especially when it comes to a new concept like mobile learning. Unfortunately, we rarely find the time to share and learn together. Whenever staff do get together, it's generally to cover "administrivia" or other collective news that could be easily shared in a large email. As we outlined in the previous chapter, learning is generally relegated to the summertime, but even then, time is so limited that we don't actually spend that time collaborating. Instead, we are usually taking the "drinking from a firehouse" approach to learning.

Collaborating can mean many things to people. According to Merriam-Webster, it means "to work with another person or group in order to achieve or do something." While this may be the true meaning of collaboration, professional learning can at times have little to do with this. Spoon-feeding information leaves little time for true collaboration, and although there is a place for step-by-step training, the modern learning environment with 24/7 access and mobile devices means that much of this can evolve. True collaboration should be interactive and truly work toward a goal of "achieving or doing something." In the next chapter I'll detail a specific formula for this I call Interactive Learning Challenges (ILCs), but in this chapter I'll cover some ways to bridge the gap between traditional methods and make them more collaborative.

Besides collaborating, one other thing traditional training fails at is celebrating and showcasing best practices among our own teachers. Sure, we might share a couple of exemplars from the classroom, but in general, our teachers teach in an isolated environment. Unlike other professions such as law or medicine, the educational industry has been built around the one-room schoolhouse model: a single teacher in control of a single room, without much time or need to share with others. Technology is breaking down many of those walls (virtually) thanks in large part to the sharing that happens on social media. Celebrating and sharing the great things teachers are doing within our organizations should be part of any professional learning plan. We'll discuss some ideas for how to highlight those everyday superstars in a mobile learning environment.

Team Planning Time

As I mentioned just now, many other professions spend time collaborating, discussing, and strategizing plans and goals for their various organizations. In an educational environment, that time can be used for a great many things, but almost by default it's spent looking over data or talking about curriculum alignment. These are important things to cover, but much like faculty meetings, they are low-hanging fruit that displace the time spent on more effective learning and sharing.

Some districts have instituted the professional learning community (PLC) concept in an attempt to increase the collaboration of teams. If encouraged and introduced correctly, PLCs can be powerful first steps in increasing collaboration and teamwork. However, if used incorrectly, they can be seen as a way to impose extra administrative tasks in an attempt to standardize instruction and stifle innovative ideas.

These are opportunities for sharing that shouldn't be wasted solely for administrative tasks. Although there has to be time dedicated to those tasks, keep a portion of that time sacred for learning as well. One concept that I've found really works well is taking one day a week during planning or PLC time to share something learned. Even if it's just 10 minutes to share a new app or learning theory or article, it promotes a higher level of sharing and encourages members of the team to seek out new learning techniques or things that interest them.

Mini–TED Talks for Conferences

Conferences can be a great way to expand concepts in professional learning. I've been fortunate to attend many great events, from SXSWedu in Texas, to ISTE, to Miami Device (http://miamidevice.org), and many conferences in between. As a district we send staff to a variety of events, and they usually come back fired up with ideas. However, one thing I noticed we didn't do well was share what was learned at those events.

How can we get staff to share their takeaways from conferences and events that we send them to? In the previous chapter, I mentioned the idea of "igniting a staff meeting," where teachers present an idea or concept for 5 minutes during a staff meeting. Why not take that same concept and apply it to teachers who attend a conference?

A couple of our elementary schools took this idea and ran with it, setting up "mini–TED Talks" at the beginning of each of their staff meetings. Teachers attending a conference go with the expectation that they will choose one or two concepts to share with the entire staff when they return.

This helps in three different ways:

1. It holds teachers accountable for the money spent on sending them to these events.

2. It creates an opportunity for other teachers to learn from the conference takeaways.

3. It sets an expectation that learning should be shared.

For campus or district leaders, setting these expectations as well as some guidelines will encourage the learning organization in the long run. Some guidelines to consider would be that teachers will have some slides or resources to share as part of their talk. It's also a good idea to set time limits on these talks (notice I called these "mini–TED talks"). Setting a time limit between 2 and 10 minutes means that a teacher who is nervous about sharing with peers only has to be up front presenting for a short amount of time. Another idea that promotes collaboration is having a partner or group to present with, as many districts send more than one person to conferences.

Appy Hours

As I mentioned in Chapter 6, we face a significant time famine when it comes to professional learning. Where do we find the time to discuss and collaborate, much less train on a concept? The idea of an Appy Hour originated from Lisa Johnson (http://twitter.com/techchef4u). Lisa is an innovative Educational Technologist whom we are lucky to have in our district, but before her time with us, she used the term "Appy Hour" to train her staff in Northeast ISD.

The Appy Hour event is a little more of an open training concept. We generally host these after school, with either the ed tech or the librarian as facilitator (although it can really be anyone). In our first few Appy Hours, I actually created menus (posted here: http://mrhook.it/menu) that staff could access via QR code (Figure 7.1) Once staff downloaded the menu and saved it (a covert way to show them how to save a PDF) they would test out several apps and then have roundtable discussions on how these could be applied.

Figure 7.1 Hosting an "Appy Hour"

As we began to introduce more of these, the training became more of a facilitation of conversations, as teachers really enjoyed having the time to come together to share best practices and tips. We would later use a version of something called "Speed-geeking" (think speed-dating, only with apps) where staff would spend 2 or 3 minutes introducing an app and then we would rotate to the next presentation. These are not meant as full-fledged presentations but more of an "APPiteaser," if you will. At the end, teachers could pick their favorite app featured and circle back for a more in-depth conversation with the teacher who was using it in class. While these aren't meant to be in-depth trainings, they do model some of the student-centered learning we want happening in classrooms. Some teachers even duplicated this approach with their students as a beginning of the year "app orientation" where students give demonstrations of particular standard apps for all students to learn. You could even take this a step further and have students do the demos on video as a kind of app tutorial catalogue for all new students and teachers.

Blog Showcases and Online Portfolios

"What do I have to blog about? When do I even have time to blog?" These are questions that often come up about blogging. I'll delve deeper in to the powerful, reflective nature of blogging in the final chapter, but sharing your experiences online or curating an online portfolio can also be useful ways to extend learning. One of the things I ask all of my team of ed techs to do is manage some sort of online presence for sharing the stories on their campus. I realize that convincing teachers to use their valuable free time to blog can be a challenge, and certain teachers will complain that they aren't good writers.

In many of our schools, teachers maintain a monthly or weekly blog with some general updates on what's happening in class. Think about how powerful that would be as a leader to leverage all of those voices to help improve learning and sharing? Just like the mini-TED talks, a blog could be used to recap concepts learned at a conference. Blogs could be used as a way to reflect on learning opportunities that went well and those that didn't go so well.

It's also best to lay out some consistent guidelines and expectations when trying to promote blogging as

BRAIN BREAK

Knife and Fork

Materials Needed: None

Concept: Working together in a teamlike charade challenge. Promotes collaboration, teamwork and creativity

Audience Size: 10–40

Set-up: Starting in partners, have teams act out several objects that come in twos (like knife and fork, boot and sock, rose and vase). Then have partners join other partners and create larger objects with four people (like car, boat, table and chair). Continue combining groups and making bigger objects until you have the entire group together to make a huge object (the Eiffel Tower, Stonehenge, etc.).

a way to share. Here are five points I'd throw out there, if you are trying to get your staff or someone on your staff to blog as a way of sharing knowledge:

1. **Follow other blogs.** There are a ton of great educational blogs out there. A great place to find a list to start following would be the Edublogs 2015 blog award winners: http://mrhook.it/blogs

2. **Tell the story**. While lists are great ways to get other people to read your blog (check out my "Top 10 Reasons I Don't Like Top 10 Lists posts" here: http://mrhook.it/list10, it's the story that ultimate becomes the sizzle that sells the steak. Keep them brief, and don't share student names without permission. But humanizing something you are doing in an actual classroom gives it more voice.

3. **Be consistent.** Make it a point to post regularly. That can mean either once a month or weekly. I try to post at least two times a month, but if you are just starting out, you might want to be be more stringent on how regularly you post.

4. **Keep it authentic.** Needless to say, these stories should be your own, or shared from a classroom that you visited or a teacher you helped. Just be careful to always ask first before sharing, or you run the risk of people thinking you are using them just for your next story.

5. **Tell the truth.** It's through failure that we learn. If you only share the successes, your message will become less believable and thus hurt your credibility.

Here are a few examples of blogs that our campus Educational Technologists have maintained through the years as ways to showcase the great things teachers in our schools are accomplishing:

Bobcat Blog: www.bobcatblog.com

WIFI Blog: http://eaneswifi.blogspot.com

The Mustang Blo: http://eedsmith.weebly.com/mustang-blog

Spearhead Ed Tech: http://edublogs.eanesisd.net/kmitchell/

Interactive Newsletters

Newsletters have been a part of schools since the early 1900s, when printing became feasible even in education. At some point in the late 1990s and early 2000s, this evolved into a "digital newsletter," which was essentially an email with the PDF version of the paper newsletter. In some cases the paper newsletter also went home in the students' weekly folders.

There are some inherent issues with either the paper form or the PDF form of a newsletter. For one, it's not very interactive. Sure, you can put links in a PDF, but how many leaders and teachers are going to have the time to do all of that? Another issue is that you can't really see who's opening it, who's reading it, and what they are reading or clicking on.

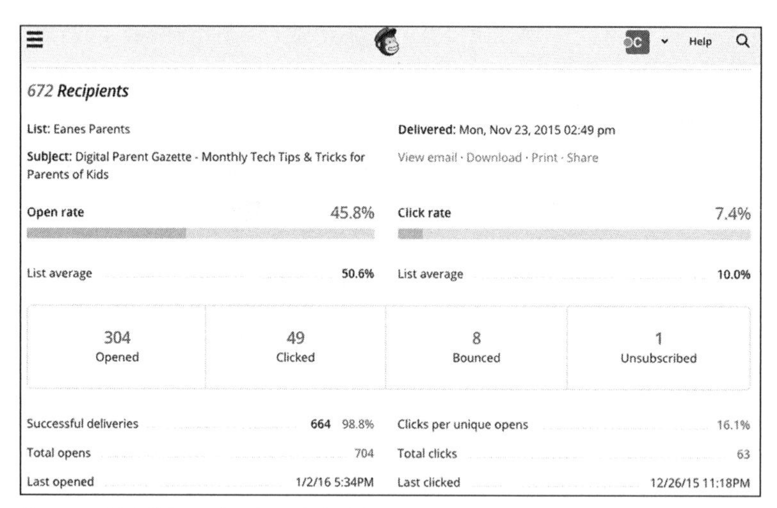

Figure 7.2 MailChimp back-end statistics

Although the blog I mentioned above could solve this issue, there are some great tools out there that can take the concept of a digital newsletter and make it more interactive and give you better statistics (Figure 7.2). One I like to use is MailChimp (http://mailchimp.com). It's a free service for up to 5,000 subscribers and gives you great data such as open rates, which readers are clicking the most, which links are being clicked on the most, and so on. I also like the drag-and-drop functionality of the templates contained within and the fact that it gives you a mobile-friendly preview. Having a service like this can allow you to increase communication to another level beyond the plain old newsletter, but without the public nature of a blog entry.

Social Media

As I've mentioned throughout this book, using social media like Twitter as a way to share and collaborate best ideas is powerful. Why should a teacher use social media? Imagine you are sitting in a room filled with thousands of other great educators. If you want to be able to tap the collective knowledge of the room, you need either a microphone or some sort of social media tool. These tools can be used not only to share information, but also as a way to curate resources for future use.

Pinterest is a rapidly growing social media platform that is essentially an online bookmarking site. However, you can share your pins with others following you or search for boards around a certain topic you are trying to teach. One of the most popular boards is maintained by good friend and colleague Lisa Johnson (http://pinterest.com/techchef4u). I've mentioned the Tech Chef before. She takes curating of resources to the next level—especially if you visit her "iPad Lessons" board (https://www.pinterest.com/techchef4u/ipad-lessons/), which has more than 16,000 followers.

For those looking for a similar bookmarking or curating concept but without all the redecorating ideas or cute pictures of kids' birthday parties, Scoop.it (http://scoop.it) is a similar approach to Pinterest. Scoop.it pages can be synced with other social media accounts, and they allow you to add a paragraph or two of feedback about each post you are "scooping." As with Pinterest, you can search through other people's posts and find similar articles and resources that you want to share. One of my most popular pages is on digital parenting and the young brain (http://mrhook.it/scoop). I often use it to curate articles for later sharing. Many of the articles I save on here I put into talks or in my Digital Parenting Gazette, an online newsletter that runs off the MailChimp engine mentioned in the previous section. The Gazette features news stories and articles about how kids think (view past articles here: http://mrhook.it/past), and using a tool like Pinterest or scoop.it, I'm able to quickly save resources and articles as I come across them.

I'd be remiss if I didn't mention the use of Twitter as a way of sharing best practices in the classroom, and specifically using Twitter with hashtags. There are hundreds of different "twitter chats" out there that use a variety of hashtags to curate their questions or information. Some of my favorites include #mathchat, #engchat, #kinderchat, and #1stchat. These and many more are used by people all over the world to post interesting tidbits or research for the world to see. Check out the giant master list that "Cybrary Man" Jerry Blumengarten has curated on his site: http://cybraryman.com.

Learning Festivals

In 2012, we were in the process of wrapping up our first year piloting 1:1 iPads when a few us began to discuss a way to celebrate and share some of the great things happening in our classrooms. We also wanted a way for teachers to have customizable choices for the training they were receiving.

As more of the team began discussing the idea of an "iConference" of sorts, we also were contemplating all the things we didn't like about conferences. They were scheduled, "sit 'n' get" type sessions with little breaks in between. In many ways they mirrored secondary classrooms. We also knew that we weren't on an island when it came to mobile learning initiatives.

In February 2012, we launched the concept of a "learning festival" of sorts called iPadpalooza. (http://ipadpalooza.com) This learning festival was centered around celebrating the shift in education that mobile learning had brought to the classroom. Other districts wanting to attend would also be encouraged to present and share some of their own learning. While we followed some formats similar to those you'd find at a conference, we also included more opportunities to collaborate and share.

In subsequent iPadpalooza events, we would introduce staggered scheduling for presentations, different styles of presentations, live music, food trucks, and a grand interactive learning challenge known as the Appmazing Race. Add in some inspiring keynote speakers from inside and outside of education, and you start to see that this isn't your normal, everyday technology conference.

So why share this idea? And how can it help schools embarking on their own mobile learning initiatives? The great thing about this concept is that it can be easily replicated and done at any level. There are actually nearly a dozen spinoffs of the original iPadpalooza, and many other schools and districts are hosting their own similar events such as iEngage Berwyn (http://www.iengage-berwyn.com) and Miami Device (http://miamidevice.org).

The core of these learning festivals is to encourage collaboration on a large scale. They give teachers reasons to share and, in some cases, even get them to try new things in their classrooms when it comes to mobile learning. Getting peers to open up and share ideas via social media, learning festivals, blogs, or good, old-fashioned face-to-face conversation will help move a mobile learning initiative past the early adoptive stages to full-fledged implementation.

INTERACTIVE LEARNING CHALLENGES

Over the course of my 16 years in public education, I've always been fascinated with how professional development gets organized and is distributed. The majority of professional development in schools happens in the short burst of summer when the kids are away and when (in theory) teachers can improve on their practice. In general, professional development is distributed either by a company or by administrators—even by other teachers on occasion. This is done over the course of a day, with a break for lunch, and involves a lot of sitting by the participants as they consume the content they are supposed to learn.

A few months later, the teacher is standing in front of their classroom and is now charged with implementing whatever strategies or content were delivered to their brain back in June. While this model of professional "learning" (the updated term, rather than "development") has been the tried and true version of adult education in the past half-century, it's loaded with flaws and ineffectiveness when it's used in the modern classroom (and world).

We preach how "student-centered" and collaborative we want the classrooms to be for students, yet we contradict ourselves by how we engage staff in professional learning. As I've mentioned throughout this book, mobile devices shift much of what happens in the classroom, and the same should be said for professional learning. This chapter is dedicated to a new strategy I call "Interactive Learning Challenges" (ILCs) that involve mobility, collaboration, creativity, and … maybe even a little bit of fun.

The APPmazing Race

At the 2014 version of iPadpalooza, we stumbled on an idea that may change the way professional learning in educational technology takes place from now on. During the three-day "learning festival," attendees were encouraged to create teams either before or during registration. These teams would take part in a 36-hour challenge known as the APPmazing Race (thanks to the clever Lisa Johnson for the title). The inspiration behind this concept was that learning takes place everywhere and anywhere, so why should we limit it to the individual sessions during the event? What about the time in between?

More than 40 teams took part in the inaugural race, and 18 actually completed all the challenges, which ranged from taking selfies with the vendors to creating a digital poster of what they ate from the infamous food trailers. (A list of challenges is shared below.) The race combined collaboration, interaction, problem solving, movement, and creation all at once. Add to that, there was no direct training on actual technology or apps. Although each and every challenge required technology, it was almost invisible at the same time.

Needless to say, the APPmazing Race was a big hit with attendees, and it got me thinking—why couldn't we do this same thing with regular, everyday staff development?

APPMAZING RACE CHALLENGE LIST FROM 2014 IPADPALOOZA

1. **Create.** A logo and team name for your team
2. **Listen.** Create a 15–20 second audio podcast that summarizes your favorite session. (background music/sound effects for a bonus point)
3. **Connect.** One team member must make a new friend from somewhere else (not on their team) and find 3 things they have in common. Create a Thinglink to represent your new friend and the 3 things you have in common. (Bonus point for finding someone from a different state or country)
4. **Sneak.** A team member photo-bombs an Eanes iVenger (hint: they will be wearing red crew shirts on Wednesday) Clarification: A proper photo bomb is when someone sneaks into a photo from behind.
5. **Capture.** Take 5 selfies with vendors and post to Instagram with hashtag #iplza14 and your team name. Capture all 5 for final submission video. 1 point per selfie.
6. **Eat.** Create a Canva poster based on your favorite food item from the food trucks.
7. **Draw.** Using a drawing app, create your best caricature of another team member.
8. **Challenge.** Create and post a Vine of a team member asking a presenter a question. (please don't interrupt a session just for this—that could result in a deduction)
9. **Outreach.** Connect with someone over FaceTime who is not at the event and show them around. Take a screenshot that displays evidence you are here.
10. **Share.** Upload and share your final video submission somewhere visible on the web. Your final video must be no longer than 2 minutes.

The Interactive Learning Challenge

"Learning by doing" is not a new concept by any stretch. However, what has changed is how we all now have access to the world in our pocket. So, armed with the success of the APPmazing Race, I've spent the past 2 years developing and testing the Interactive Learning Challenge concept.

At its core, an Interactive Learning Challenge starts with the concepts of collaborative problem solving and interactive creativity, and adds an element of competition to learning. An ILC can take place over the course of several days or even in an hour. It can be done with as few as a dozen people or as many as a few hundred (as was the case at iPadpalooza).

I debuted the Interactive Learning Challenge to a group of 150 staff members at a school in San Antonio, Texas. Their superintendent had contacted me about delivering a keynote speech during their "Welcome Back" convocation. He then mentioned that if I wanted, instead of the typical hour for a keynote, I could have two and a half hours to expand it into some sort of interactive workshop. This was the perfect time to try out my theory.

After setting the tone for the day, I had the entire group line up and self-identify who was the most or least tech-savvy. After that, I paired and grouped the staff to ensure that each team of four included at least one "high tech" person. The way I designed the challenges, every team member had to participate in the creation of the final product, regardless of tech skills. Rather than confine them to the lecture hall, I placed challenges throughout the building. Completing one challenge revealed the clue to another, and so on. One staff member called it a "scavenger hunt on steroids."

Every group completed the challenge, and after we reconvened, I asked the staff to reflect on what they had completed. Some of the takeaways were that they loved moving while they learned, and that those who had self-identified as least tech-savvy felt empowered and actually learned some apps they hadn't known before. Needless to say, it was a huge success, and many of them send me messages even today about how engaging and interactive it was, but more importantly, about how they are trying the same thing with their kids in class.

While I don't think this style of staff development can be applied to all topics, I'm working on making a series of "recipes" based on subject matter, group size, device availability, and timeframe so that others can try this same approach to professional learning. My hope isn't so much for Interactive Learning Challenges to revolutionize the way we do professional development around technology as much as it is to maximize the time we have for learning.

And it doesn't hurt if the learning is also fun, right?

Before we dive into the concept of Interactive Learning Challenges, let's dissect the traditional training model to see where the inefficiencies of learning lie and how what I'm proposing will improve those, making the learning much more meaningful and applicable. I'll break the discussion into the following four areas: Content, Space, Time, and Delivery.

Content

In the pre-21st century model of learning, content was created by a publisher, edited, and distributed by an "educational company." This company was made up of industry experts who sifted and determined what content should be shared and taught to both teachers and students.

In the current professional development setting, the content is still the primary driver of adult learning. Have some new math standards or a textbook that was just adopted? We need to spend 2 days sitting and listening to a hired gun from the publisher as they go over each unit, strand, or learning standard in painstaking fashion. Sure, there might be some time at the end of the second day to look at your own units in the upcoming year and how you might align those with this new content, but for the most part, the content is hand-delivered to your brain without much room for remixing.

Space

The traditional professional development space is typically in rows or maybe a "cabaret" style table setting (as seen in Figure 8.1) The thinking behind the latter arrangement is to foster some discussion throughout the course of the day, thus checking off the "collaboration" box when the day is over. This format is a marked improvement over sitting in rows as if at a faculty meeting or lecture, but it still could use some improvement. Most districts lack an official professional development space, so the use of libraries, computer labs, or even cafeterias comes into play. Even with the round table setup, these spaces are limited in many ways by the furniture, lighting, and even colors on the walls. With the addition of modern technology such as an A/V projector, the space can be retrofitted to make it more modern, but generally it's going to be an inflexible and depressing place.

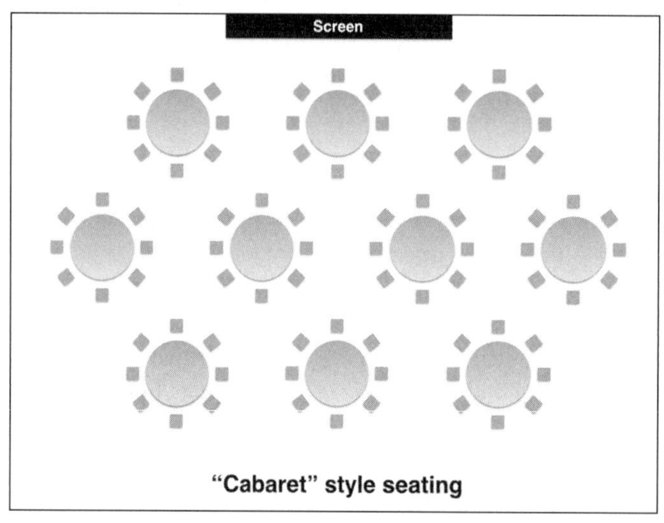

Figure 8.1 "Cabaret" style seating

When it comes to how and where teachers sit in these environments, it's usually with friends or colleagues who teach the same subject. This gives them a chance to catch up on personal conversations and work with people they work with on a daily basis. It does in fact, encourage the growth of an echo chamber when it comes to dynamic, outside-the-box thinking. In these group settings, roles have already been established, and a dominant team member will carry the majority of the day's workload should they be asked to do any type of group activity. The more quiet members of the table can sit back and check their Facebook status, do some online shopping, or go ahead with some menial task that "just needs to get done" such as cutting out letters or some sort of bulletin board art.

Time

As I stated earlier, the majority of professional development takes place in full-day bursts over the course of a summer (primarily in June). The day is usually split into two 3-hour chunks with a 45-minute to 1-hour lunch break in between. A teacher sitting through the 6 hours of training will be honored with some continuing education (CE) credit and be able to check off a box during their evaluation that they completed some level of training in math, technology, writing, and so on. While this makes the teacher feel like more of an adult in terms of time management, what generally happens is that teachers show up a little late or leave early or even take a longer lunch by a few minutes, thus cutting into any "learning" time throughout the day. The person tasked with delivering the content usually feels compelled to let the attendees out a little early, too, especially when the blank stares and yawns start to appear around 3:00 p.m. Just like that, you've lost an hour of "learning" time in this traditional method.

When professional learning takes place on the calendar has been changing, but it still primarily resides in the middle of summer or generally the first 2 weeks *after* the school year ends, or 1 week *before* the school year begins. The idea is, let's cram as much of this content down when teachers are still around and school is either fresh in their brain or is pressing on their minds as the kids prepare to walk through the doors in a matter of days.

The major flaws with having professional learning during those times of year may not be so obvious at first, but bear with me here.

If you are a teacher who has just completed a 180-day school year, a year packed with classroom management, technology struggles, and testing stresses, your brain is ready for a vacation more than it is to absorb new content. Districts generally feel like having those first 2 weeks of summer reserved for professional learning guarantees that teachers will not only have time to digest the new content, they'll have time to figure out how to integrate it into the coming school year, which is only 12 weeks away. So now you have an overwhelmed, exhausted educator who has just been spoon-fed loads of new information and then asked to retain and implement it a few months later.

The alternative schedule for professional learning is the week before school starts. The rationale there is that teachers have had a full 2 to 3 months to digest, reflect, and put the past year behind them and are now refreshed and ready to start the year anew. I do see that this time of year carries more optimism than the first few weeks of summer. Even teachers with a stressful previous school year have generally forgotten some of the pain, so it won't cloud their perception of new content or knowledge. However, the biggest fault with this time of year is the fact it's set only a few days before kids enter the building. Most teachers are stressed, worrying about setting up their classroom or designing their lessons for the first few weeks. A teacher fretting about those things while sitting in a 6-hour PD session won't have the capacity to be perceptive about anything new, especially if it's just hand-delivered to them. The chance of implementing anything new is also at risk because most teachers have already planned out various units and activities, so introducing new content into that set plan represents more work and last-minute adjustment.

Delivery

So, knowing that teachers only have a short burst of time, usually in the summer, to download so much content, professional development turns into a passive activity. The attendee's role is that of a consumer of the content, while the facilitator's role is delivering the material in a matter that is memorable so that teachers can use it in the next year. The good news is that much of the professional development I've attended in the past 5 to 7 years has been shifting from the lecture delivery method to that of a mixture of mini-lecture/discussion/activity.

It seems like the "Learning Pyramid" (Figure 8.2) that has been around since the 1970s is finally gaining some traction in the professional development arena. Lecture, A/V, discussion, and practice help with the learner's retention of material. While the discussion can add to that retention, it's generally centered around a prompt rather than an actual project to collaborate around. The majority of the work done involves the brain, the eyes, the ears, and the mouth. Hands are left idle with the possible exception of writing down something on a poster board that the group was prompted to summarize.

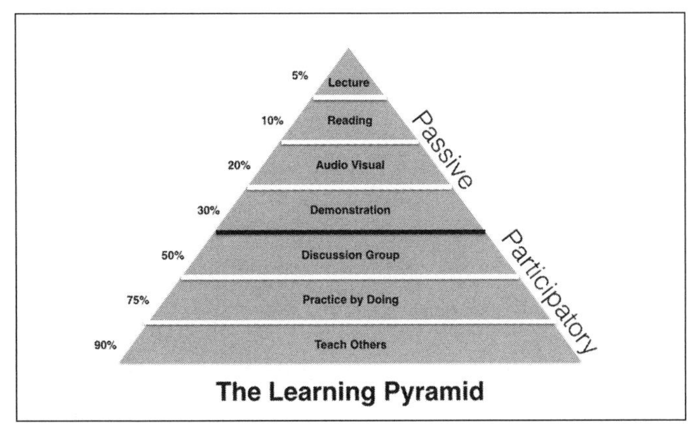

Figure 8.2 The Learning Pyramid. Based on research from National Training Laboratories

Goals and Outcomes

The focus of any professional learning is to have the attendees learn a new activity, standard, or content, and then apply that new material to their classroom practice. I've sat in many a professional learning presentation or workshop where they've preached how we need to make the learning more student-centered—yet the workshop is far from student-centered.

I think there is a better way to get the classroom teacher to absorb and use new content. A way that is truly student-centered and can take place in 1 hour after school, over the course of a day in the summer, or (ideally) throughout the entire school year. It is with that thought in mind, and an awareness of all the difficulties I've just discussed, that I designed these Interactive Learning Challenges. Mobile technology has given us learning in the palm of our hands, yet we don't use it fully in our professional learning sessions. Sure, some sessions have a backchannel like a TodaysMeet (http://todaysmeet.com) or maybe an interactive quiz or prompt using a tool like Socrative (http://m.socrative.com) or Kahoot! (http://getkahoot.com). However, these same tasks can be done in a sit-down, traditional computer lab setting as well. With the world at our fingertips and wireless, why do we still feel the need to tether ourselves to a desk or table? The idea behind ILCs is not only to use mobile devices, but to make them essential to completing the challenges.

Realizing fully the constraints of the traditional professional development setting of content, space, time, and delivery, I've spent time creating several different "recipes" of challenges depending on the amount of time you have, the types of devices you have access to, and the groups you'll be working with. Although I won't go into these recipes with too much depth, I do expect to publish my ILC recipe book at some point in the future.

That said, I will give you the general setup for these and let your creativity take over from there. For the most part the challenges are device agnostic, but they generally require one member of the team to have a device that can take pictures and video, record sound, and access the internet. Luckily, with smartphone technology, most learners have access to these tools.

The ILCs are also designed around the concept of true group collaboration. If only one member of the group has a mobile device, it can still be an effective and productive group. Although competition does play a role in the challenges, the primary goal is to have *every* group complete a challenge and have time to reflect on it. The other goal is to encourage teachers to use this same type of student-centered, mobile learning in their classrooms. It takes a lot to change the traditional teaching pedagogy, even in a 1:1 environment. A district trying to use the strategies behind ILCs should realistically ask that teachers attempt to do at least one of these in the course of a semester with a class or subject.

Grouping Strategies

A company such as Google sees the benefits of heterogenous grouping when it comes to fostering collaboration and innovation. When they started out, being an online company, they were big believers that employees could work remotely from home. However, what ended up happening was that collaboration began to decrease. When people did come to the office, they would take lunches with the same group of people and rarely break from their team.

Google realized that in order to increase collaboration (and innovation), people from different fields needed to be put into situations where conversation and learning was happening. They began to make small changes, starting with creating "micro-kitchens" where food and drinks were free for employees. They also created smaller conference rooms for groups to collaborate on projects together. The final step was making lunch free, but also setting up long tables cafeteria-style settings so that people couldn't just sit with the same four people. The result was situations where a communications person would be chatting with a database manager about how terrible email is to use and as a result … Gmail was born.

Teachers in a professional learning environment also generally group with people they know. They find comfort in those they know, so this is a natural behavior. However, it can also create a bit of an echo chamber and not stretch people's thinking. Learning and growth comes from overcoming challenges and getting a bit out of your comfort zone, so being with a group of people you know well makes that harder to accomplish.

Before assigning team members and beginning the challenges, you will want to consider what you are trying to accomplish. For some groups, you might want to make the teams self-selected to keep teachers within their comfort zone in at least one aspect. One thing I like to do is have each person self-identify their tech savvy-ness on a scale of weakest to strongest. Once they form a line and sort themselves out in some sort of order, I fold the line in half and make sure that the most tech-savvy is partnered up with the least. They can either partner up at that point or make sets of partners next to each other form a group of four.

Some other ideas I've seen work:

1. Preassign random objects that belong in triads or fours on the back of people's badges. Then, have everyone try and find others in their group. So you might have a group that is primary colors and the three staff members get blue, red, or yellow on their badges. They have to find each other and without knowing the commonality. Another example would be putting "Ringo, John, Paul, George" on the backs of four badges so they have to find their group, the Beatles.

2. Line everyone up and have them count off up to a number you specify, and repeat. This works well when you have fewer than 40 people. Then all the "1s" get together, then the "2s," and so on.

3. If you don't like the ability-grouping lineup suggested, you could have them line up by birthdate—only do it without talking. Always makes for an interesting ice-breaker. When done, fold the line in half and create the teams of two or four as before.

Distributing Challenges

Giving out the challenges can be almost as much fun as what the teams actually turn in. With the first iPadpalooza example in Table 8.1, I just emailed the team captain the list at the beginning. Teams could break up the challenges into different parts and delegate who does what based on the difficulty of the challenges.

A method I've come to favor over the years is using Google Docs as a way to distribute challenges. That way I can always change the back end of the challenges in case something goes amiss, and it refreshes in real-time. Doing this in an email or a PDF makes it static—and, as we all know with technology, things can fail even with the best planning. I can either send the team the entire list like Table 8.1, or I can use my favorite method, which is giving them an opening QR code that takes them to the first challenge, and then that links to the next, and the next, and so on. Here is an example list of challenges on a Google doc: http://mrhook.it/list

Probably the most fun version of this would be to make QR codes for each challenge and hide them throughout the building. This makes it into a bit of a scavenger hunt and gets people moving throughout the building. If you link the QR codes to the Google docs, as I mentioned earlier, you can still change the content without breaking the links if something doesn't work. The one word of caution with this is to make sure your custodial crew is aware that you are doing this. I once set up a race like this before lunch, and when we came back, the custodians had removed all the posters throughout the building!

Some other ideas for distributing challenges:

1. Set up a challenge website that you could update with new challenges throughout the day.
2. Use a group texting service such as "Group Me" or Google Hangouts to send them out throughout the day.
3. If you have a district or conference app, you could use that as a way for people to use the app and get the challenges.
4. Tweet the challenges out to a certain hashtag at different times. Using a tool like Tweetdeck (http://tweetdeck.com), you could schedule the tweets to come out at certain times. This has the added bonus of getting staff on social media and possibly seeing some of the power behind it.

Gathering Learning Artifacts

Now that staff have created teams and have a way of getting the challenges, they'll need a place to turn in their finished work. Challenges can range from taking a selfie with a known landmark around the school to creating an interactive video explaining a simple physics concept using animation. Regardless of the challenges, you'll want to make sure there is a simple way for teams to "turn in" their learning artifacts as they complete them.

Luckily, with the web, there can be many different ways to do this, depending on your timeframe. One of my favorite tools to use for gathering the learning artifacts they create is using a tool like Padlet (http://padlet.com). Padlet works out well because it's completely web-based and can be accessed from any device that gets to the web. So if you have a team that has many different devices, they can still post on their team Padlet wall from anywhere and from any device. A word of advice—make the creation of the Padlet team wall the very first challenge, and have teams share the link to their wall with you. This way you can actually watch them virtually complete challenges as they post them on their virtual walls.

Some other ways to "gather" the learning artifacts they create:

1. Create a shared Google Drive folder for each team to use. (Bonus points here if you are trying to get your staff to use Google more often.)

2. Use an existing learning management system that your school uses.

3. Have them tweet their completed challenges to an assigned hashtag.

4. Have the teams create a video showing all the challenges completed and upload to YouTube or similar video service. Their final project is a video that shows them finishing each challenge. This is what we did in 2014 at iPadpalooza. and it was a great way to show completed challenges—but make sure you leave time at the end to create the videos. Here's an example of one of the winning teams: http://mrhook.it/racers

Reflection and Celebration

Completing an Interactive Learning Challenge can be a great, powerful way to showcase teamwork and mobility. Regardless of how you try to run your ILC, make sure that you build in time at the end, not only to showcase the winning or completed teams, but also to reflect on the process. This reflection time can come in handy when you are scoring the teams or gathering videos to showcase.

Here are some questions I like to ask:

1. How could a challenge like this be used in the classroom? What subject areas?

2. How else could you use this challenge for Professional Development?

3. How were the concepts of creativity and collaboration used during the challenge?

4. What are some other ideas that would be useful to add to this challenge?

In the end, you'll have some great artifacts that you can showcase throughout the year, and in the best case, teachers will start to apply these concepts of mobility, interaction, and creativity in the classroom.

BRAIN BREAK

"Alpha-Bits"

Materials Needed: None

Concept: Creative thinking through storytelling in alphabetic sequence

Audience Size: Any size

Setup: Working in partners, have each person tell one sentence of a story. The only rule is that each sentence must begin with a sequential letter in the alphabet. For an extra challenge, time the groups and see who makes it to the letter Z, or have them start with Z and work backward.

Example: Describe a fictitious vacation that you two went on a few years ago. Now retell the story starting with the letter A. Partner A: "All my friends don't believe that trip to Brazil we took last year." Partner B: "Be sure to not share the part that happened on the beach." Partner A: "Come on! I would never tell them that." Partner B: "Don't!", and so on and so on.

TYING IT ALL TOGETHER: PROFESSIONAL LEARNING WITH ALL GROUPS

As with every book in this series, it's important to see where everything fits in the mobile learning initiative. Professional learning is a major piece of the puzzle that affects all groups within the learning community to varying degrees. Teachers and campus leaders need to see the value in the professional learning that accompanies a mobile learning initiative, and the district leadership needs to find the time and money to provide it. The technology department has to coordinate what will be needed to make the technology work successfully. Parents not only need to see the value in it for staff—they should also play the role of learner at times during a parent workshop or training.

Here's a deeper dive in the interconnected roles each of these groups plays in making professional learning successful in a mobile learning initiative.

Teachers and Environment

If the classroom is all about student learning, then professional learning should be all about the teachers and educators in the building. They need to be valued but also see the value in the training events they are attending. Teachers should be actively looking for takeaways for their own classroom and for ways to participate. Having some small goals when walking into a training and then reflecting on those goals can make it much more meaningful. Whenever I attend a session at a conference or a district training, I try to take away at least one item that I can learn from to help with my professional growth.

Teaching adults can be much more difficult than teaching kids. Teachers have the burden of thinking of their own classroom, their daily life, their kids, their spouse, and so on. All of this is in their heads when they enter a room to learn from you. Just like their students, each teacher also comes with their own set of learning styles. Be sure to design professional learning that offers some flexibility in those styles. Some teachers may like step-by-step instructions, while others may want to fly ahead. Some may like working in teams, while others may want to work alone. Although you might not be able to accommodate all styles, allow for some flexibility when you can.

The environment should be comfortable and flexible as well. Most districts don't have the benefit of an adult professional learning space, so much of it takes place in libraries, cafeterias, computer labs, and classrooms. Try and make sure the space is well-lit and the temperature is at a good level. These may seem like minor things, but the environment can greatly affect attention and retention as learning.

Campus Leaders

Campus leaders not only need to see the value of professional learning, they need to be an active part of it. The principal has so many hats that often the "instructional leader" hat falls by the wayside and is replaced by the "parent communicator" hat or the "building financial officer" hat, among others. It's so important for building leaders to be active participants in learning not only to model adult learning, but also to show that they believe in what is being trained so strongly that they are willing to put all their other hats away to learn alongside staff.

Professional learning should be embedded throughout the year and be a part of the teachers' growth. During the evaluation cycle, identify areas of growth with staff, but also provide suggestions for professional learning that will help the staff improve on weaknesses. As a leader, you should also identify staff members who have strengths and encourage them to lead the professional learning on a particular topic. This not only builds capacity, it also showcases the many great things teachers are doing in the classroom on a daily basis.

Feed them and they will learn. I know that the first thing to go during budget setbacks is the professional development food budget, but I'd ask that you reconsider this as a building leader. Whenever I've personally attended a great workshop or all-day training, I've found that the ones that provide food seem to be the most successful. Think of Maslow's hierarchy of needs (http://mrhook.it/maslow). Before you can even begin to feel loved or self-actualize, you need to take care of physiological needs like air and hunger. A hungry brain doesn't learn well. It would be well worth the $5 bag of variety chocolate to keep your staff active and engaged in learning.

District Leaders

District leaders have the most direct effect on professional learning in a district. They are the ones who control the time and money dedicated to staff growth. In the case of mobile devices, I've been a witness to far too many districts purchasing devices and not accounting for the training that needs to come with them. I call it the "gift with a tail."

One infamous case of this happened in a district that shall remain nameless. They spent millions of dollars to purchase some 20,000 netbooks and carts to distribute to their many campuses. However, they provided no initial training or follow-up, so the district ended up with millions of dollars in devices collecting dust in closets. Even districts that distribute technology with some initial training will not get very far without follow-up training, support, and time for staff to collaborate on challenges and provide feedback.

When constructing and planning professional development for staff, it's important to make sure that all stakeholders have a voice in the offerings. I've seen districts spend thousands of dollars to bring in speakers or put on an event that is mandatory for staff to attend, but the staff never gets any say in the event or the learning. There should be a level of buy-in and interest when preparing these events for staff.

I do realize at some point there might be a training that isn't something they are personally interested in, but that may be part of larger district goal or mission. In those situations, consider a variety of ways to present the information or to have the staff interact with it. Just because it's a mandatory training on blood-borne pathogens doesn't mean everyone has to sit through a 20-minute presentation. Why not put that online? If a textbook company has a new set of tools that staff need to be aware of, why not set up a series of challenges like the ILCs in Chapter 8 rather than force people to sit and listen for 3 to 6 hours?

Finally, as I'll discuss in the final chapter, make sure there is a way for staff to provide feedback to whatever training is offered. It not only reinforces the idea behind reflection, but it shows that district leaders are also trying to improve (assuming they actually read and respond to the feedback). Showing that you are listening to their input and feedback will strengthen the bond between district and campus staff and provide leaders with good ideas for improving adult learning.

Technology Department

A technology department rolling out mobile devices to hundreds or thousands of students and staff can often be overwhelmed in the summer, when most professional learning takes place. That doesn't mean they have an easy out when it comes to avoiding or not supporting it. At one of our biggest events (iPadpalooza, mentioned earlier), our technology department always makes sure to have three or four staff members on hand to handle the challenges that may arise throughout the day. They make adjustments to Wi-Fi settings for out-of-district guests and check all the projectors where sessions are taking place.

This level of support should be the norm in a district that truly values professional learning. IN an analogy to Maslow's hierarchy, it's awfully hard to provide successful training, especially about mobile devices, if the wireless doesn't work or technology is broken. Campus and district leaders should be in constant communication with the technology department about upcoming training offerings and the technology needed to make it successful.

I'd also add that just like staff and leaders, technology department staff should also value the professional learning and seek out ways to improve their practice. No other field is changing as rapidly as technology, and having a team that avoids learning new strategies or skills can mean stagnation in terms of support. A district that places a strong value on the learning of the adults should promote that learning for every staff member in the organization, including the technology department.

Parents

Finally, parent involvement in professional learning shouldn't be an afterthought. District and campus leaders should be constantly communicating the importance and results of professional learning to the community. I've been involved in focus group conversations with parents about professional learning, and some don't see the value of it right away. They just see it as "another time my child's teacher is absent" or another expense that could go to something more important.

A parent community that believes in professional learning will also support it financially. With educational budgets tight in many states, having a booster club or PTO that supports the professional learning by paying for a conference for staff or bringing in a speaker can be extremely valuable. This only happens with communication between the district leaders and community members about the goals and objectives of the district. It just so happens that a great time to have that conversation is when the district is rolling out mobile devices to students for the first time or launching a BYOD-type initiative.

I'd also throw in here that parent education should not be an underestimated part of a successful mobile device initiative. Students will spend more time away from campus with their devices than on campus (if they are taking them home), yet many districts don't provide support for parents other than a flyer or FAQ page.

I value this group and their learning so much that I've dedicated an entire book to the learning and collaboration of the parent community during a mobile device initiative. Parent learning can happen during the school day, during a portion of a booster club meeting, or even during a parent-teacher conference. Many districts provide some level of mandatory parent orientation when first introducing mobile devices to help with ideas for home and to handle questions.

I started professional learning with parents in the most familiar format, face to face, but as the initiative continued, I added in other components. One was hosting a parent panel discussion (http://mrhook.it/panel), where community members had conversations about mobile learning and tools they could use to help with it at home. The other was offering an online course for parents to take (http://mrhook.it/101—only available on iOS at the moment) so that they could be learning along side their kids using a mobile device.

As I've shown here, communicating the importance of professional learning is more than a one-way conversation. Each area has certain needs and wants when it comes to professional learning, but certain parts of it need to be non-negotiable if you trying to create a cultural shift toward learning with mobile devices.

Teachers *need* to respect and believe in what they are taking the time to learn. Parents *need* to see that it has direct impact on their child's learning. The technology department *needs* to value providing support for it as a top priority. District leaders *need* to constantly be seeking growth and feedback on their offerings for professional learning, as well as communicating its importance throughout the organization. Campus leaders *need* to create an atmosphere in their building where professional learning is valued by all their staff and a part of professional growth.

Without these needs met, professional learning could just become an afterthought.

CHAPTER 10

REFLECTING TO LEARN AND LEARNING TO REFLECT

I'm never short on "great" ideas when it comes to education. I put "great" in quotes because, one, I'm not so egotistical that I truly believe that, and two, although I think they may be great, they often don't pan out. I had an idea like that the first time I tried to develop an online learning course for staff.

In 2013, I was working with a couple of educational students from the local university on developing an online course for teachers. Although they were dedicated to the project, I never communicated a clear vision of what I wanted the learning outcomes to be. I gave them tidbits of tasks to create and put in the platform, but when I stepped back and looked at the final product, it was disjointed and full of flaws. There was no way for teachers to communicate or collaborate. There was no way to hand in completed projects.

It was a mess, but because I was under a time crunch, I put it out there anyway.

When it was finished, I sent out a survey to the 20 brave souls who volunteered to be a part of that first online learning endeavor. As you can imagine, much of the feedback was negative—but one positive thing was common in all their feedback. Teachers enjoyed being able to learn on their own and at their own pace. This reinforced that the concept was good even though the delivery was poor.

Reflecting on learning can be almost as powerful as the learning itself. If I hadn't taken the time to ask for feedback and reflect on my mistakes, I might have continued to put out a bad product, or maybe scrapped the idea altogether as a waste of time. The teachers who participated also gained much out of it, despite its flaws, and actually liked the idea of learning this way.

In the classroom, with the steady stream of content that we are trying to get through with our students, reflection is often left out. Because it usually happens at the end of a unit or project, it's left on the cutting-room floor, sacrificed to the educational gods, as teachers feel the time crunch to get onto the next subject. But it doesn't always have to be that way. In this final chapter, I reflect (ironically) on ways to use reflection throughout professional learning and how mobile devices can make this even more a part of the everyday learning process.

"Fist to Five"

One of my favorite, low-tech ways to check for understanding and feedback is the "fist to five" method. I first saw this in action during a workshop led by educational consultant Greg Kulowiec (@gregkulowiec—http://twitter.com/gregkulowiec). He mentioned to me that he had learned of the method during a Skype debate between his class and a fellow history teacher, Shawn McCusker (@ShawnMcCusker—http://twitter.com/ShawnMcCusker).

As he was about to introduce a new tool or concept, he asked the audience to rate their prior knowledge of the tool or concept—using their hands. A "fist" (or zero) would represent no knowledge whatsoever about what was about to be taught, and all five fingers meant that they knew it so well they could teach it.

This is a great way to gauge audience knowledge so that you aren't wasting their time covering the basics of a tool that everyone knows or showing advanced uses of tool to an audience that doesn't even know what it is. After differentiating and delivering his lesson based on their initial "fist to five" feedback, he would then ask them to reflect how much their rating had changed now that the lesson was over. Inevitably "fists" would become twos or threes, and those who started as threes or fours would move up to five.

But he wouldn't stop there. For his own feedback, he would then ask them for a second fist to five rating. He asked the attendees to rate how useful and applicable the information they learned would be in their classroom. This feedback response not only made the audience think about application of the concept in the classroom, it also gave Greg feedback on how he could adjust the lesson going forward. Imagine that happening in a class that repeats throughout the day. The teacher introducing the concept to the first period class would have refined the lesson throughout so that by the time the seventh period class entered the room, the teacher would have a finely polished lesson to deliver (lucky for them!).

Live Journaling

Taking notes, either with paper and pencil or typing, can help internalize what is being learned. Applying and using those notes later can sometimes be challenging, especially if you are trying to teach others based on your chicken-scratch writing. "Live journaling" throughout a training session or conference can be valuable for retaining and also sharing what was learned. Here are four tools that I've used either personally or during professional learning to help with live journaling:

Evernote. The online note-taking app can be used on any device and can even capture audio and photos to drop right into the notes. Because it lives in the cloud, you can access it from anywhere and share it with anyone.

Google Docs. Keeping notes during an extremely engaging and interactive training can be a challenge. Why not share the load and do some collaborative note-taking? One of the best training sessions I ever attended was the Apple Academy for administrators in Cupertino, California. It was 5 days long and was a model way to deliver professional learning. Even though it was so great, it actually became even more powerful because of the way I took notes. Myself and two other participants decided to share a Google doc at the beginning of the training and document the activities, drop in example links and images, and set up a timeline for delivery. That way we could return to our own districts and use the parts we learned to train others.

Twitter Hashtag. I know what you are thinking. Isn't Twitter a social media tool? One of the most useful parts of Twitter for learning is using a hashtag to curate information. Whenever I attend a conference or learning event, I post things I've learned on a specific hashtag. If the event has an official hashtag, I'll post there, but I can also make up my own to circle back to at a later date.

Book Creator. If you are truly trying to make an artifact to take back with you and share with others, one of the best tools I've used is Book Creator (http://www.redjumper.net/bookcreator/). It's an app available on most mobile platforms that lets you create a book containing all of your experiences. I've used it with my own daughter to reflect on our yearly summer road trip, and I've used it with a room full of educators to reflect on specific parts of their learning journey. It allows you to drop in video, audio, pictures, drawing, and text onto separate pages. You can then publish your final book in an ePub format for others to read or for you to return to and reflect on.

Sketchnoting

I've always been drawn toward art (see what I did there?). I took drafting and art classes throughout my educational upbringing. But strangely enough, I left all of that behind when I entered college. The concept of taking notes using art, or "sketchnoting," first came to my attention when I noticed Educational Consultant Tracy Clark (@tracyclark08—http://twitter.com/tracyclark08) sketching out a drawing on her notepad during Sugata Mitra's keynote address at iPadpalooza. When I looked at her finished masterpiece, I was amazed at how much of his talk she was able to capture in visual form. (She blogged about the experience here: http://mrhook.it/sketch.)

Figure 10.1 My Sketchnotes for Sugata Mitra's keynote, created using the Paper app.

Inspired by her and this new method of note-taking, plus the added excuse of being allowed to doodle while I listen, I began to do my own sketchnotes during presentations. Using the Paper app by FiftyThree (www.fiftythree.com) and a stylus, I was able to digitally capture and retain much more than I ever had before. While my art still leaves much to the imagination (Figure 10.1), I can still go back and look at these drawings and remember what was said in much greater detail than I would if I were reading written notes.

Podcasting

Taking the concept of visual feedback and reflection in sketchnoting to a different medium, podcasts can be another way to capture learning. With mobile devices, it's become much easier to record our spoken thoughts and post them for others to hear.

One of the best at this is Adam Jones (@adamjonesed—http://twitter.com/adamjonesed). Adam is Educational Technology Director at the Proctor Academy in New Hampshire, and when he travels to other conferences, he'll use his iPhone and microphone to capture his thinking. He used this technique during the 2015 iPadpalooza, not only to help himself reflect, but also to let others in on his experience. Listen to his educational podcasts and reflection here: http://mrhook.it/podcast.

Backchannels

Just as taking collaborative notes via a Google doc can be valuable for reflection, using a backchannel to capture learning can be a good way to "see" what your audience is thinking as well as curate questions. Providing a backchannel to your audience keeps them more engaged in the learning and gives them an avenue to think and ponder out loud. Here are my three favorite methods for creating and using a backchannel.

Hashtags. I've used Twitter hashtags to curate resources and capture my own ideas, but I also like to use them during presentations and professional learning as a way to capture thinking and pose questions to the audience. Because these are on social media, you get the added benefit of having people from around the world answering your questions, making it a truly global learning event. One thing I like to remind staff who attend professional learning with a Twitter backchannel is that it doesn't just exist for me. They are encouraged to revisit the hashtag and reflect on what was discussed and learned.

TodaysMeet. (http://todaysmeet.com) TodaysMeet was one of the first tools I ever discovered that was completely web-based and required no login. The downside of that is that it can also be used to post thoughts and musings anonymously, which can be a temptation for middle school students to post inappropriate phrases (this goes for athletic coaches, too, strangely enough).

BRAIN BREAK

Love/Hate

Materials Needed: None

Concept: Discuss differences of opinions using physical movement to decide if you love or hate a topic

Audience Size: 10+

Set-up: Have several different topics ready to discuss. Explain to the group that one side of the room is the "love" side and the other is the "hate" side. Then show the topic on a slide and have the attendees chose sides. If they are indifferent or in the middle, they can stand in the middle. Then have the groups turn and discuss why they are standing where they are standing. Change the subject and watch the room shift.

Example topics: Some favorite topics here would be "professional development," or "school boards," or "assessment." I also like to warm them up with things like "Reality TV" or "Facebook" as topics.

That said, the rooms "expire" after a certain timeframe and can be another way to encourage feedback at the end of a session by asking attendees to post one thing they learned or one major takeaway from their professional learning experience.

Padlet. (http://padlet.com) I've mentioned using Padlet to gather challenges during an ILC (Chapter 8), but my first experience with these interactive online walls was in using them to post feedback and to pose questions as a backchannel. Here's one I used at a recent workshop with the title "I used to think but now I think" for attendees to reflect on what they had learned that day: http://padlet.com/chooker/iLeap

Blogging

We all learn from each other. Many of my biggest failings and successes I've shared on my blog (http://hookedoninnovation.com). Blogging is very similar to the live journaling concept, except that it's for the entire world to see and experience. Although not every teacher may want to share their thoughts with the world, there is something powerful about seeing that your learning affected someone from another state or country.

One idea for getting this to happen with staff is to try it on something small at first. If you are introducing a new concept with mobile devices, or perhaps a new app to try out in a lesson, reflect on how the experience went for you. What things would you improve? Was it effective for student learning? Would you do this lesson again? These are all great reflective questions to ask, and by answering them "out loud" in a blog, you can share with colleagues and the world so that they can celebrate and learn from your idea.

Blackmailing Yourself

With the way the school yearly schedule breaks down, much professional learning happens during the summer months when the students are not in the building. This means that when school starts up again in August or September, much of what was learned over the summer was lost. You may have attended an amazing training full of great ideas, but a couple of months later, you're left looking through old notes or trying to find a handout so you can jog your memory.

A great method for reflection and recall is doing what I call "blackmailing" yourself. Using a tool like FutureMe.org (http://futureme.org) you can actually send your future self an email. When I complete a training, I ask the staff to reflect on some of their favorite takeaways and to send them in an email timed to arrive in the first week or so of school.

A way to do this with a bit more structure is using the "Three 5's" method. The "Three 5's" is a prompt for attendees to reflect on what they have learned and for brainstorming ideas that they can put into action in the first 5 days of class, the first 5 weeks, and the first 5 months. The ideas usually range from something simple implemented in the first 5 days to a bigger goal or project that will be attempted in the first 5 months. Writing these ideas down when they learn them and then sending them to their future self creates a feeling of revisited excitement around the concept when it pops back into their inbox some months later.

All of the methods outlined in this chapter were included for a reason. If we truly want to move the needle with the professional learning that we are encouraging staff to attend, and if we want to invest money and time into our staff learning and growing, then we need to continually reflect. It's through this reflection that we become better facilitators of learning in our organization. It's through this reflection that our students will benefit from ideas that we didn't even conceive possible. It's through this reflection that our mobile device initiative will improve, grow, and change the ways our students learn now and in the future.

ISTE STANDARDS

The ISTE Standards for Coaches (ISTE Standards•C)

All technology coaches should be prepared to meet the following standards and performance indicators.

1. Visionary Leadership

Technology Coaches inspire and participate in the development and implementation of a shared vision for the comprehensive integration of technology to promote excellence and support transformational change throughout the instructional environment. Technology Coaches:

- **a.** contribute to the development, communication, and implementation
  of a shared vision for the comprehensive use of technology to support a digital-age education for all students
- **b.** contribute to the planning, development, communication, implementation, and evaluation of technology-infused strategic plans at the district and school levels
- **c.** advocate for policies, procedures, programs, and funding strategies to support implementation of the shared vision represented in the school and district technology plans and guidelines
- **d.** implement strategies for initiating and sustaining technology innovations and manage the change process in schools and classrooms

2. Teaching, Learning, and Assessments

Technology Coaches assist teachers in using technology effectively for assessing student learning, differentiating instruction, and providing rigorous, relevant, and engaging learning experiences for all students. Technology Coaches:

- **a.** Coach teachers in and model design and implementation of technology enhanced learning experiences addressing content standards and student technology standards
- **b.** Coach teachers in and model design and implementation of technology-enhanced learning experiences using a variety of research-based, learner-centered instructional strategies and assessment tools to address the diverse needs and interests of all students
- **c.** Coach teachers in and model engagement of students in local and global interdisciplinary units in which technology helps students assume professional roles, research real-world problems, collaborate with others, and produce products that are meaningful and useful to a wide audience
- **d.** Coach teachers in and model design and implementation of technology-enhanced learning experiences emphasizing creativity, higher-order thinking skills and processes, and mental habits of mind (e.g., critical thinking, metacognition, and self-regulation)
- **e.** Coach teachers in and model design and implementation of technology-enhanced learning experiences using differentiation, including adjusting content, process, product, and learning environment based upon student readiness levels, learning styles, interests, and personal goals
- **f.** Coach teachers in and model incorporation of research-based best practices in instructional design when planning technology-enhanced learning experiences

g. Coach teachers in and model effective use of technology tools and resources to continuously assess student learning and technology literacy by applying a rich variety of formative and summative assessments aligned with content and student technology standards

h. Coach teachers in and model effective use of technology tools and resources to systematically collect and analyze student achievement data, interpret results, and communicate findings to improve instructional practice and maximize student learning

3. Digital Age Learning Environments

Technology coaches create and support effective digital-age learning environments to maximize the learning of all students. Technology Coaches:

a. Model effective classroom management and collaborative learning strategies to maximize teacher and student use of digital tools and resources and access to technology-rich learning environments

b. Maintain and manage a variety of digital tools and resources for teacher and student use in technology-rich learning environments

c. Coach teachers in and model use of online and blended learning, digital content, and collaborative learning networks to support and extend student learning as well as expand opportunities and choices for online professional development for teachers and administrators

d. Select, evaluate, and facilitate the use of adaptive and assistive technologies to support student learning

e. Troubleshoot basic software, hardware, and connectivity problems common in digital learning environments

f. Collaborate with teachers and administrators to select and evaluate digital tools and resources that enhance teaching and learning and are compatible with the school technology infrastructure

g. Use digital communication and collaboration tools to communicate locally and globally with students, parents, peers, and the larger community

4. Professional Development and Program Evaluation

Technology coaches conduct needs assessments, develop technology-related professional learning programs, and evaluate the impact on instructional practice and student learning. Technology Coaches:

a. Conduct needs assessments to inform the content and delivery of technology-related professional learning programs that result in a positive impact on student learning

b. Design, develop, and implement technology-rich professional learning programs that model principles of adult learning and promote digital-age best practices in teaching, learning, and assessment

c. Evaluate results of professional learning programs to determine the effectiveness on deepening teacher content knowledge, improving teacher pedagogical skills, and/or increasing student learning

5. Digital Citizenship

Technology coaches model and promote digital citizenship. Technology Coaches:

a. Model and promote strategies for achieving equitable access to digital tools and resources and technology-related best practices for all students and teachers

b. Model and facilitate safe, healthy, legal, and ethical uses of digital information and technologies

c. Model and promote diversity, cultural understanding, and global awareness by using digital-age communication and collaboration tools to interact locally and globally with students, peers, parents, and the larger community

6. Content Knowledge and Professional Growth

Technology coaches demonstrate professional knowledge, skills, and dispositions in content, pedagogical, and technological areas as well as adult learning and leadership and are continuously deepening their knowledge and expertise. Technology Coaches:

- **a.** Engage in continual learning to deepen content and pedagogical knowledge in technology integration and current and emerging technologies necessary to effectively implement the ISTE Standards•S and ISTE Standards•T
- **b.** Engage in continuous learning to deepen professional knowledge, skills, and dispositions in organizational change and leadership, project management, and adult learning to improve professional practice
- **c.** Regularly evaluate and reflect on their professional practice and dispositions to improve and strengthen their ability to effectively model and facilitate technology-enhanced learning experiences

REFERENCES

Blumengarten, J. (n.d.). Cybrary man's educational web sites: Some educational hashtags. Retrieved from http://cybraryman.com/edhashtags.html

Clark, T. (2014). Playing with sketchnotes: Sugata Mitra keynote [Web log post]. Retrieved from http://tracyannclark.com/2014/07/25/playing-with-sketchnotes-sugata-mitra-keynote/

Diamond, D. (2013). Just 8% of people achieve their New Year's resolutions. Here's how they do it. Retrieved from http://www.forbes.com/sites/dandiamond/2013/01/01/just-8-of-people-achieve-their-new-years-resolutions-heres-how-they-did-it/

DuFour, R., DuFour, R., Eaker, R., & Many, T. (2006). *Learning by doing: A handbook for professional learning communities at work.* Bloomington, IN: Solution Tree

Eanes ISD WIFI Project Site. (2015). WIFI project gets started: iPad launch day August 24 [Web log post]. http://eaneswifi.blogspot.com/2011/09/wifi-pilot-gets-started.html)

Fullan, M. (2001). *Leading in a culture of change.* Retrieved from http://www.csus.edu/indiv/j/jelinekd/edte%20227/fullanleadinginacultureofchange.pdf

Hooker, C. (2014) How does staffing affect technology support? [Web log post]. Retrieved from http://hookedoninnovation.com/2014/12/19/how-does-staffing-affect-technology-integration-support/

Hooker, C. (2013). Taking a dip in the SAMR swimming pool [Web log post]. Retrieved from http://hookedoninnovation.com/2013/12/10/taking-a-dip-in-the-samr-swimming-pool/

Hooker, C. (2014). The best app for monitoring students [Web log post]. Retrieved from http://hookedoninnovation.com/2014/02/24/the-best-app-for-monitoring-students/

Hooker, C. (2015). Edutopia blog post: It's time to make learning fun again … even for adults [Web log post]. Retrieved from http://www.edutopia.org/blog/make-learning-fun-for-adults-carl-hooker

Hooker, C. (2014). The APPMazing Race: A great way to increase collaboration and learning at an event [Web log post]. Retrieved from http://hookedoninnovation.com/2014/07/01/the-appmazing-race-a-great-way-to-increase-collaboration-and-learning-at-an-event/

Laura Wright's Third Grade Class. (2013). *The life of an Eanes pioneer child* [iTunes version]. Retrieved from https://itunes.apple.com/us/book/life-eanes-pioneer-child/id595702755?mt=11

L.E.A.P. Initiative by Eanes ISD. (2015). Learning and engaging through access and personalization. The Eanes ISD 1:1 iPad Initiative. Retrieved from https://eanesisd.net/leap

Maslow, A. (1943). A theory of human motivation. *Psychological Review. 50(*4)

Muhammad, A. (2009). Transforming school culture: How to overcome staff division. Bloomington, IN: Solution Tree

National Training Laboratories. (n.d). The learning pyramid. Retrieved from http://www.ntl.org/

Niche. (2015). Best K–12 schools: 2015 Niche rankings. Retrieved from https://k12.niche.com/westlake-high-school-austin-tx

Project RED. (n.d.). About Project RED. Retrieved from http://one-to-oneinstitute.org/about

Puentadura, R. (n.d.). *SAMR: Methods for transforming the classroom.* Retrieved from http://www.hippasus.com/rrpweblog/archives/2013/10/25/SAMR_MethodsForTransformingTheClassroom.pdf

Schrock, K (n.d.) *Kathy Schrock's guide to everything.* Retrieved from http://www.schrockguide.net/

Sinek, S. (2009). TED Talk: How great leaders inspire action. Retrieved from http://www.ted.com/talks/simon_sinek_how_great_leaders_inspire_action

TPACK. (2011). What is TPACK? Retrieved from http://www.tpack.org